Growing New Ventures, Creating New Jobs

This book is one of a series titled **Entrepreneurship: Principles and Practices** sponsored by the Center for Entrepreneurial Leadership Inc. of the Ewing Marion Kauffman Foundation. The series merges the experiences of successful entrepreneurs with the applied research of leading scholars. It seeks to combine the best practices of entrepreneurs with the relevant, useful and impactful findings of leading scholars. The series thus provides an opportunity to increase our understanding of the entrepreneurial process by focusing on the factors that help entrepreneurs succeed.

TITLES IN THE SERIES

Growing New Ventures, Creating New Jobs: Principles & Practices of Successful Business Incubation, by Mark Rice and Jana B. Matthews.

The Entrepreneur as Leader: Personal and Organizational Development in Entrepreneurial Ventures, edited by Donald L. Sexton and Raymond W. Smilor.

Growing New Ventures, Creating New Jobs

Principles & Practices of Successful Business Incubation

Mark P. Rice and Jana B. Matthews

Contributing Authors
**Laura Kilcrease, Susan Matlock,
Robert Meeder, Julius Morgan,
and Robert Sherwood**

Entrepreneurship: Principles and Practices

Prepared under the auspices of the
Center for Entrepreneurial Leadership Inc.

Q
QUORUM BOOKS
Westport, Connecticut • London

Library of Congress Cataloging-in-Publication Data

Rice, Mark P.
    Growing new ventures, creating new jobs : principles & practices
of successful business incubation / Mark P. Rice and Jana B.
Matthews ; contributing authors, Laura Kilcrease . . . [et al.].
    p. cm. — (Entrepreneurship, principles and practices, ISSN
1083–334X)
    "Prepared under the auspices of the Center for Entrepreneurial
Leadership, Inc."
    Includes bibliographical references and index.
    ISBN 1–56720–033–8 (alk. paper)
    1. Business incubators.   2. Entrepreneurship.   3. Job creation.
4. Leadership. 5. Management.   I. Matthews, Jana B.
II. Kilcrease, Laura.   III. Title. IV. Series.
HD62.5.R53   1995
658.4—dc20   95–34541

British Library Cataloguing in Publication Data is available.

Library of Congress Catalog Card Number: 95-34541
ISBN: 1–56720–033–8
ISSN: 1083–334X

First published in 1995

Quorum Books, 88 Post Road West, Westport, CT 06881
An imprint of Greenwood Publishing Group, Inc.

Printed in the United States of America

The paper used in this book complies with the
Permanent Paper Standard issued by the National
Information Standards Organization (Z39.48–1984).

10 9 8 7 6 5 4 3 2 1

"By highlighting the 'best practices' of business incubators and their presidents, *Growing New Ventures, Creating New Jobs* provides an invaluable resource to those committed to cultivating entrepreneurs."

– **Ted Gaebler, The Gaebler Group;**
Author of *Reinventing Government*

"The development of new entrepreneurial ventures is the bedrock on which communities will build economic vitality in the future. Rice and Matthews give definitive guidance to incubator sponsors and managers to meet the goal of helping entrepreneurs succeed."

– **James Morgan, General Partner, OneLiberty Ventures;**
President, National Venture Capital Association

"*Growing New Ventures, Creating New Jobs* will be an indispensable handbook for any organization or individual launching or operating a business incubator. It explains every facet of how to make an incubator successful and achieve the greatest economic return for its sponsoring community."

– **Christopher M. Coburn, Vice President,**
Technology Partnership Practice, Battelle Institute;
Editor and Co-author, *Partnerships: A Compendium*
of State and Federal Cooperative Technology Programs

"A draft of this publication served as our road map during the planning of our new business incubator. It will be the definitive publication on the structuring and operation of business incubators for years to come."

– **Ivan Smith, President,**
JoCo Business Tech Center

"In straightforward language, *Growing New Ventures, Creating New Jobs* provides a blueprint for establishing a business incubator ... it gives new direction and vision to those in the business incubator industry."

– **Gregory K. Ericksen, National Director,**
Entrepreneurial Services, Ernst & Young, LLP

"In the next century, every community's survival will depend on its ability to foster new entrepreneurial companies. This book is a practical road map to new business incubation."

– **Robert A. Compton, General Partner,**
CID Equity Partners

"In our industry of increasing competitiveness, difficult downsizing, rising consumer expectations, and high requirements for return-on-investment, Matthews and Rice's analysis of best practices and guiding principles for business incubators is right on target."

– Donna M. Auguste, Senior Director,
US West Advanced Technologies

"A superb guide to success in nurturing entrepreneurial ventures. It addresses the vital issues of starting and operating a venture incubator – and of avoiding the pitfalls! Entrepreneurs, too, will benefit from this book's insights and advice."

– Roland Schmitt, President Emeritus,
Rensselaer Polytechnic Institute; former Senior Vice President,
Science & Technology, General Electric Corp.

"Business incubators have been experiencing most of the start-up problems that the companies they are creating are experiencing. This book defines critical success factors that will help existing and new incubators. It is MUST reading for those involved with incubators."

– Earl McLaughlin, Vice President, Retail Energy Services,
Public Service Company of Colorado

"Jana Matthews and Mark Rice have collected a great deal of real-world experience and 'best practices' which will save people a lot of time and money."

– David J. BenDaniel,
Johnson Graduate School of Management,
Cornell University

"Matthews and Rice's *Growing New Ventures, Creating New Jobs* is a MUST for anyone who wants to learn more about or practice the process of incubation. The authors have provided practical and priceless insights to help entrepreneurs succeed in growing companies."

– Dr. George Kozmetsky, Director, IC^2 Institute,
The University of Texas at Austin

"This book emphasizes the practical results of mission orientation in incubator management."

– Teri F. Willey, Purdue Research Foundation,
Office of Technology Transfer

"Reading *Growing New Ventures, Creating New Jobs* proved to me that my experience as a successful entrepreneur did not necessarily qualify me to be part of an incubator management team. This book has proven to be an invaluable source of information that would have otherwise taken me years of trial and error to learn."

– Joe Edwards, JoCo Business Tech Center

"*Growing New Ventures, Creating New Jobs* will make a real contribution to molding the mission and policies of the University's technology incubator and research park planned for the Pease International Tradeport."

– Wm. E. Wetzel Jr., Director Emeritus,
Center for Venture Research,
University of New Hampshire

"The authors have helped hundreds of entrepreneurs, and their combined wisdom is captured in this easy-to-read guide for sponsors, presidents and other stakeholders of business assistance programs."

– Michael Marvin, Chairman, MapInfo Corporation;
Principal, Exponential Business Development Company

"This book is must reading for anyone who thinks starting a venture incubator could be a panacea for regional economic problems. Drs. Matthews and Rice accurately describe many of the pitfalls of incubators and the complex role they play in job and wealth creation."

– John T. Preston, Director of Technology Development,
Massachusetts Institute of Technology

"The investment behind a technology incubator and the potential community rewards are both too high to risk a trial and error approach. *Growing New Ventures, Creating New Jobs* came along just at the right moment to help us avoid making fatal mistakes."

– Marcia B. Mellitz, Director, Missouri Innovation Center

"We could have avoided making mistakes through the discovery process if a copy of this book was available when our incubator began. It is an excellent guide for building a successful business incubator."

– Richard A. Bendis, President,
Kansas Technology Enterprise Corporation

Contents

Chapter 3: Understanding the Financial Dynamics of Incubators   21

Chapter 4: Establishing Roles & Responsibilities of the Board   47

Chapter 5: Managing the Stakeholder Network   65

Chapter 6: Building the Incubator Management Team   73

Chapter 7: Selecting the Optimal Incubator Facility   85

Chapter 8: Recruiting & Selecting Client Companies   95

Chapter 9: Making the Difference: Serving Client Needs   113

Chapter 10: Beyond Incubators: Emerging Trends & Strategies for Business Incubation   133

Figures

Acknowledgments

This book is the result of a collaboration between the Center for Entrepreneurial Leadership Inc. at the Ewing Marion Kauffman Foundation and the Center for Entrepreneurship of New Technological Ventures at Rensselaer Polytechnic Institute. We asked five other distinguished incubator directors and presidents to help identify and describe the principles and practices outlined in this book: Laura Kilcrease, Director of the Austin Technology Incubator; Susan Matlock, Executive Director of the Birmingham Business Assistance Network; Dr. Robert Meeder, President of SPEDD, Inc.; Julius Morgan, Director of Entrepreneurial Development & Training of the Milwaukee Enterprise Center; and Robert Sherwood, President of the Center for Business Innovation, Inc. The collective experience of this group includes many years of hands-on experience with the development and management of successful incubators. We are grateful to the contributing authors and to all others who reviewed drafts of the manuscript and offered ideas and suggestions. In addition, we appreciate the encouragement and support provided by our colleagues and families throughout the writing of this book.

Mark P. Rice, *Troy, New York*
Jana B. Matthews, *Kansas City, Missouri*

Preface

When Ewing Marion Kauffman created the Center for Entrepreneurial Leadership Inc. at the Ewing Marion Kauffman Foundation in 1992, he had one outcome in mind—job creation. But he understood that jobs, indeed economic development, depended on the ability of entrepreneurs to grow companies. He was convinced that the best way to enhance the possibilities of success for entrepreneurs was to identify and teach the skills that contribute to entrepreneurial development. If entrepreneurs could learn how to develop successful companies, jobs would be created, as surely as the day follows the night. And these jobs would be one way the Ewing Marion Kauffman Foundation could achieve its mission: *"self-sufficient people in healthy communities."*

Mr. Kauffman was the consummate entrepreneur. He founded Marion Laboratories in 1950 with $5,000. When that company was merged with Merrell Dow in 1989, it was valued by the NYSE at more than $6 billion and employed over 3,000 people. Mr. K, as he was known, knew from this personal experience that entrepreneurs are critical to the economy. Thus his vision of the Center for Entrepreneurial Leadership Inc., included entrepreneurial support systems, and he recognized the importance of business incubators in the development of start-up companies.

Although the Center for Entrepreneurial Leadership Inc. does not plan to operate an incubator, the board and staff have a keen interest in how incubators work, what they do and how they should be developed and managed. Because the Center believes well-conceived and managed incubators are powerful support systems for entrepreneurs, it provided funding to underwrite the development of this book. For the first time, the principles and practices of successful business incubation are clearly identified and outlined in detail. Incubators based on the principles and practices in this book will achieve their mission: the growth of successful companies. They will also become hubs for entrepreneurial activity and catalysts for the development of start-up companies in their communities. Hence, business incubators and successful business incubation programs stimulate the creation and development of entrepreneurs and entrepreneurial ventures—which form the bedrock on which healthy communities can be built and people can become self-sufficient.

Introduction

Communities all over America are trying to understand and replicate the development that has occurred along Route 128 and in Silicon Valley. What "magic" causes clusters of companies to spring up, as if overnight, grow fast and create thousands of jobs? What support systems, what entrepreneurial infrastructures should communities develop to help companies grow?

The economic landscape is populated with all sorts of business incubation programs: business incubators, small business development centers, technology transfer programs, training programs for women and minority enterprises, small business investment companies, angel networks—to name a few. It is important to understand that many of the principles and practices discussed in this book can be applied to all these business incubation programs. However, this book specifically focuses on business incubators because they are at the forefront of this emerging trend of "support systems" for entrepreneurs and new venture creation. The number of incubators has been expanding at a phenomenal rate—from 10 in 1980 to approximately 500 in 1994—and a new incubator is opening every week.

From the data available, the National Business Incubation Association (NBIA) extrapolates that incubators have helped create at least 82,000 jobs. This figure assumes an average of 140 jobs created per incubator, a figure derived from responses to a 1991 NBIA survey. The NBIA believes the actual number of jobs created by companies receiving assistance from incubators is closer to 100,000,[1] but the association has not had the capacity to fully document the incubator industry's growth. In the NBIA's 1995 directory, existing incubators reported about 8,000 current client companies and 4,500 companies that had graduated.

But what has been a promising experiment in economic development is

---

1 – This figure considers only jobs in the United States; incubators have also been established in many countries outside of the United States.

in danger of becoming the latest "fad." Communities are rushing to create incubators without understanding that incubators are "start-up" ventures whose purpose is the development of other start-up companies. It is difficult to imagine a more unstable situation. If newly formed incubators are not financed and managed as entrepreneurial ventures, they are in grave danger from the beginning. As a result, many incubators that were established with great hope and bright futures are now floundering because of unrealistic expectations, inadequate resources, and inappropriate governance and management structures.

After twelve years, the incubator industry has a track record that is checkered, at best. Some incubators are signal successes, others are dismal failures, and there are numerous marginal "survivors." A 1992 report published by Coopers & Lybrand, entitled *Business Incubators: Coping with the Recession*, suggests that the incubator industry is in trouble. Decreasing numbers of full-time executive directors and increasing numbers of part-time directors indicate that they are being asked to take on more functions and responsibilities in an already crowded day. Most executive directors of incubators spend little time—often less than 10% of their time—assisting client companies. Political support for incubators tends to wane after a year or two, and public subsidies dwindle. This undermines the financial stability of an incubator and distracts the president and board, who begin spending their time searching for additional funds rather than working with companies. The upshot of all this is dissatisfaction among tenant companies, sponsors and incubator directors.

Just what are incubators and what do they do? By definition an incubator is a business assistance program that provides entrepreneurs with appropriate advice and counsel and serves as a "switching center" to other people and resources, as needed. Typically, incubator programs are housed in incubator centers in which companies can co-locate, rent space and share business services and equipment. Hence incubators comprise three components: (1) a person (or staff) who provides advice/mentoring and access to a resource network; (2) shared services, which means a company located in the incubator does not have to outlay funds for a secretary, phone, fax machine and photocopying machine; and (3) flexible space, rented on a monthly basis, that can be expanded or contracted as needed.

As its name implies, the National Business Incubation Association (NBIA) recognized early on that the *process of business incubation* was much more important than the *incubator facility* within which companies co-located. However, many communities have focused on the bricks and mortar aspect of incubators to the detriment of the incubation process. An inappropriate incubator facility is a quick ticket to disaster, but a good facility is no guarantee of success. Incubator sponsors and presidents need to understand the rationale for incubators and the whole cluster of concepts that are required for their success. This book provides guidance regarding topics such as facilities, financing, staffing, governance and services. Each chapter includes examples and case studies of what to do and what not to do. This book will be useful to those responsible for economic development and incubator development; to corporations, universities and federal labs considering incubators to help commercialize shelf-technology; and to sponsors and presidents who want to reorient existing incubators in order to realize their full potential.

PARTIES-AT-INTEREST

There are many individuals and groups with an interest in the development of an incubator. The first step in the development process is to identify who the interested parties are, define their interests and describe what role they should play.

Stakeholders: Stakeholders are those parties that have an interest in the success of the incubator. Stakeholders can be divided into several subgroups, e.g., client companies, incubator staff, incubator board, sponsors, know-how network, and so forth.

Sponsors: Sponsors include individuals and organizations that contribute financially to the support of the incubator as a business. Sponsors are sometimes third parties who make contributions to the incubator, or they may serve as the parent organization for the incubator, e.g., universities, utilities, companies, economic development agencies, community organizations and governmental units. Sometimes an organization or institution may not make a financial contribution but may be such a strong advocate for the incubator that it persuades or influences other organizations to contribute; in such cases that organization may also be recognized as a sponsor.

Embedded Incubators: Sometimes an incubator may be part of a university, a company, a chamber of commerce or another larger economic development agency. In this book, this arrangement is referred to as an "embedded incubator."

Know-How Network: Another sub-group of stakeholders are experts such as lawyers, bankers, accountants, consultants, professors, technology experts and others who provide services to businesses and are willing to make these available to the incubator and its client companies free of charge or at a reduced rate. In this book, we refer to these people collectively as the Know-How Network.

Community: The community in which the incubator is located includes stakeholders and may also include other institutions and individuals who may not directly have a stake in the incubator but who may be called upon to assist the incubator or its client companies, e.g., real estate developers who own facilities into which incubator graduates may decide to move. The community is the ultimate beneficiary of a successful incubator when companies graduate from the incubator, join the business community and become new sources of economic activity and jobs.

President of the Incubator: The people who lead and manage incubators currently carry a wide variety of titles, e.g., President, Executive Director, Director and Manager. The most commonly used titles are "Executive Director" and "Director," perhaps reflecting the fact that most incubator sponsors are non-profit organizations. However, in this book we will use the title "President" to reflect the conviction of the authors that, regardless of sponsorship, incubators should be operated like businesses, and the professional staff of the incubator organization should understand they are managing a company—with customers, products, services, assets and liabilities.

Finally, this book undertakes to do more than just teach the parties-at-interest how to develop and manage successful business incubators. It provides information about the business incubation process—wherever it occurs—inside or outside an incubator facility. Several of the most successful incubators now provide services to companies outside their facility—some to companies hundreds of miles away. Hence, an understanding of the process of business incubation is essential for anyone involved with business incubators.

By describing current concepts and future trends, this book provides direction to those who want to help entrepreneurs grow successful companies. Rather than reflect common practice, the book provides a vision of best practice in the development and management of incubators. It should help correct the "drift" in the incubator industry and chart the direction to the "dream," i.e., provide a vision and direction for incubator sponsors and presidents and help them understand the "magic" of company creation, job creation and economic development.

Principles & Practices of Successful Business Incubation

ECONOMIC RESTRUCTURING

America has been jolted by massive corporate restructuring and the transition from a cold war to a peace-time economy. Some companies that were household names such as IBM and Sears have seen their stock plummet and have laid off thousands of employees; others have been merged, been acquired or ceased to exist. These changes in the economy have created major dislocations, discontinuities and uncertainties—all of which are sources of opportunities for new entrepreneurial ventures. As a result, many new companies have burst on the scene, some displaying dazzling growth, and some established companies are recognizing they must develop a capacity for entrepreneurial management to cope with a rapidly changing, highly uncertain business environment.

Academics, economists and other pundits can argue about the reasons for this economic restructuring, but the implications are clear: entrepreneurial companies have been the primary source of the net new jobs in the United States over the past decade. All indicators point toward continued high uncertainty and rapid pace of change, which in turn will require greater entrepreneurial capacity and skill in established companies, new ventures and organizations providing services to these ventures.

NEW VENTURES: PROBLEMS AND PROMISE

The difficulty of expecting new ventures to be the "drivers" of the U.S. economy is related to their instability. Start-up companies have a high failure rate. Failures include companies that are poorly planned, with products and services that are not attuned to the market. However, they also include companies with great promise and innovative products that cannot get adequate financing and need to learn how to market their products and services, develop strategic alliances and find effective distribution channels. The challenge is to identify the ventures with great promise, provide the assistance they need and help them achieve their potential—not founder and die. Incubators can be the catalyst, an important part of the "support structure," to make sure this happens, i.e., to find and screen promising ventures, give them the assistance they need and help them grow.

THREE PRINCIPLES OF INCUBATOR DEVELOPMENT

The purpose of this book is to identify the basic principles and best practices of successful incubators. Many of the published studies about the incubator industry have been based on data collected from incubators, summarized and widely reported. Others have used this data to guide their choice of buildings, compensation plans, rental rates for tenants, and so forth. The problem with this approach is that it summarizes *Common Practice* but provides no guidance about *Best Practice*. Those who structure and develop incubators based on common practice are destined to repeat the mistakes of those who have gone before them.

By combining their knowledge and experiences, the authors of this book have identified three basic principles and ten best practices of successful incubators. The three principles are outlined in Figure 1.

The First Principle of incubator development relates to its mission:

FIGURE 1

Three Principles of Successful Business Incubation

I. Focus the energy and resources of the incubator on developing companies.

II. Manage the incubator as a business, i.e., minimize the resources spent on "overhead," and develop a self-sustainable, efficient business operation.

III. Develop a sophisticated array of services and programs that can be targeted to companies, depending on their needs and stage of development.

Principle I

FOCUS THE ENERGY AND RESOURCES
OF THE INCUBATOR ON DEVELOPING COMPANIES

Many of the incubators in the United States have been established in response to economic dislocation and distress. While their goal is often job creation, too few have been able to achieve their purpose. One reason is that incubators often have multiple missions, e.g., contribute to urban redevelopment, empower various sub-groups of the population, commercialize university or corporate technology, revitalize the inner city. The "empowerment" incubators, the "neighborhood revitalization" incubators and the technology incubators will all be more successful if they focus on one goal and make the *mission of the incubator the development of companies.*

The reasoning behind this premise is simple: as companies develop they will grow and add jobs. As more employees are added, more money will be pumped into the economy, more people will become self-sufficient and more will feel empowered. Neighborhoods will be revitalized, and economic development will occur. Focusing the mission of the incubator on any purpose other than developing companies will compromise its future and viability.

The Second Principle relates to how the incubator is managed:

Principle II

MANAGE THE INCUBATOR AS A BUSINESS, I.E., MINIMIZE
THE RESOURCES SPENT ON "OVERHEAD" AND DEVELOP
A SELF-SUSTAINABLE, EFFICIENT BUSINESS OPERATION.

Recognize that the incubator, itself, is a new venture that will undergo the same trials and tribulations as a start-up company. The incubator must develop a business plan, select the right staff, secure financing and then develop and modify its services to meet the needs of its customers (client companies). Even after becoming established, incubators will still need to update their business plans, select replacement staff, manage cash flow and develop new services to meet the changing needs of their client companies. The only way to do this is to manage the incubator like a business, regardless of its legal status as a not-for-profit or for-profit entity. By doing so, the incubator will lead by example, and companies associated with the incubator will have a model to emulate.

Unfortunately, too many incubators have been conceived and managed as subsidized programs, with no attention to the concept of "bottom line." The president becomes involved in fund raising, public relations, board meetings and governance, and networking—activities which would be categorized as "overhead" in the corporate world. As a result, he/she spends very little time on developing the "product" of the incubator: successful companies.

The Third Principle relates to what the incubator does, and follows naturally from the first two principles:

Principle III

DEVELOP A SOPHISTICATED ARRAY OF SERVICES AND PROGRAMS THAT CAN BE TARGETED TO COMPANIES, DEPENDING ON THEIR NEEDS AND STAGE OF DEVELOPMENT.

In order to develop successful companies, an incubator must develop differentiated programs to meet the various needs of its customers—a "one size fits all" approach will not do. Best-practices incubators develop a flexible approach to the provision of advice, counsel and services; they have different kinds of services and programs for their client companies, and they deliver assistance in different ways, depending on each company's individual needs and stage of development.

These three core principles are basic to the development of successful incubators, regardless of whether they are inner city redevelopment mechanisms; attached to a university to facilitate technology transfer; part of a community's economic development strategy; or housed within a company to develop shelf-technology and offer an alternative to displaced employees.

TEN BEST PRACTICES

The First and Second Principles specify what the mission of the incubator should be and how it should be managed. The Third Principle summarizes what the incubator does and how it helps companies be successful. The ten best practices described in Figure 2 provide specific suggestions, dos and don'ts about how to develop an incubator that will manifest best practices.

The first best practice flows naturally out of the previous discussion of the three basic principles underlying successful business incubation. The remaining nine best practices, each described in its own chapter, are all extensions of the three principles as well. Some are focused on the most efficient and effective ways to manage an incubator, i.e., managing the business functions efficiently, thereby maximizing the resources that can be directed to the companies, thus enhancing the effectiveness of the incubator. Other best practices describe how to determine what types of assistance companies need in order to grow and develop. However, in order to develop a best-practices incubator, the first thing that must be done is to decide to develop an incubator that is based on the three core principles described above.

BEST PRACTICE #1

COMMIT TO THE CORE PRINCIPLES OF BUSINESS INCUBATION AS THE FIRST STEP IN DEVELOPING A BEST-PRACTICES BUSINESS INCUBATOR.

Following these principles and practices does not guarantee a successful incubator, but it will certainly increase the probability of developing one that helps companies grow.

FIGURE 2

Ten Best Practices

Best Practice #1: Commit to the Core Principles of Business Incubation as the First Step in Developing a Best-Practices Business Incubator

Best Practice #2: Collect and Assess Key Information. Decide Whether the Incubator is Feasible—or Not

Best Practice #3: Structure the Incubator Program to be Financially Self-Sustainable

Best Practice #4: Structure the Incubator Organization to Minimize Governance and Maximize Assistance to Incubator Companies

Best Practice #5: Engage Stakeholders to Help Companies and to Support Incubator Operations

Best Practice #6: Recruit Staff Who Will Manage the Incubator Like a Business and a President Who Has the Capacity to Help Companies Grow

Best Practice #7: Choose a Building That Will Enable the Incubator to Generate Sufficient Revenue and Also Support Business Incubation

Best Practice #8: Recruit and Select Client Companies That Provide Revenue Required in the Financial Model and Have the Potential to Grow and Create Jobs

Best Practice #9: Customize the Delivery of Assistance and Address the Developmental Needs of Each Company

Best Practice #10: Engage in Continual Evaluation and Improvement as the Incubator Progresses Through Various Stages of Development and as the Needs of Client Companies Change Over Time

ORGANIZATION OF THIS BOOK

Just as the entrepreneur needs to answer a set of questions before starting a new business, those involved in incubator development need to answer the same types of questions:

- Is this idea, i.e., an incubator, feasible?
- How will the incubator be financed?
- What kinds of management skills are needed and what characteristics are essential in the person who assumes the role of president of the incubator?
- Is there a market for the products or services the incubator could provide?
- What specific products or services are needed in order to meet the needs of the market, i.e., entrepreneurs who want to affiliate with an incubator in order to grow their companies more successfully?

The sequence of chapters in this book is designed to enable the reader to address these questions and answer them in a systematic fashion. For example, Chapter 2 addresses the issues of feasibility straight-on. The chapter is entitled, "To Be or Not To Be: Determining Incubator Feasibility." Too many incubators have been started after someone hears about the concept of incubators, donates a facility or simply decides to set up an incubator. A best-practices incubator will begin with a feasibility study, and the decision about whether to proceed or not will be based on a thorough and objective analysis of the information gathered through this process.

The latest NBIA State of the Industry Survey identified financing the incubator as the number one challenge facing incubators. This issue is considered in Chapter 3: "Understanding the Financial Dynamics of Incubators," and to some extent in Chapter 7: "Selecting the Optimal Incubator Facility." For most incubators, a large proportion of revenue is derived from leasing or sub-leasing portions of space in the overall facility to client companies who are tenants. With a substantial proportion of its revenue dependent on start-up companies that may not have enough money to pay rent or may be late paying rent, many incubators experience severe cash flow problems. Hence, understanding the sources and uses of funds to support the incubator and its mission is crucial.

Building a team for success—including selecting and structuring the governing board, managing the stakeholder network, and selecting the incubator president and staff—are the topics of three key chapters in the middle of the book: Chapter 4: "Establishing Roles and Responsibilities of the Board;" Chapter 5: "Managing the Stakeholder Network;" Chapter 6: "Building the Incubator Management Team."

Chapters 8 and 9 focus on the customers, the client companies and the markets for business incubation services. Understanding how to identify, stimulate and tap into appropriate markets of companies to create the right client company mix is the subject of Chapter 8: "Recruiting and Selecting Client Companies." Managing the development and delivery of programs, resources and services to meet the needs of individual companies at various stages of their development is the focus of Chapter 9: "Making the Difference: Serving Client Needs." The final chapter, Chapter 10: "Beyond Incubators: Emerging Trends and Strategies for Business Incubation," identifies some other issues that impinge on the development of new ventures and job creation and suggests additional strategies that could lead to more successful incubation programs.

2

To Be or Not to Be: Determining Incubator Feasibility

It is all too common practice for incubator sponsors to charge ahead and establish an incubator without first conducting an adequate feasibility study. Consequently, they do not understand the business incubation process and are likely to make critical errors of judgment and planning that result in an incubator that can only be characterized as "marginal" at best.

On the other hand, most incubators require entrepreneurs to submit a business plan as part of the incubator admissions process. The founding sponsors of an incubator need to think of themselves as entrepreneurs trying to launch a new business, i.e., a business incubator. They, too, need to invest time and capital in doing a feasibility study, thereby laying the groundwork for their incubator's business plan.

BEST PRACTICE #2

COLLECT AND ASSESS KEY INFORMATION. DECIDE WHETHER THE INCUBATOR IS FEASIBLE—OR NOT

A feasibility study allows sponsors to understand the climate for business incubation in their community, the market for services the incubator proposes to provide, and the commitments necessary to develop a viable program. With sufficient due diligence, sponsors can reach an intelligent decision regarding whether their incubator is "to be or not to be." If they decide to proceed, the feasibility study provides a basis for making subsequent decisions required for a successful program launch. Sponsors should consider the following ten steps when designing their feasibility study.

IDENTIFY AND UNDERSTAND THE MARKET

As is the case for any entrepreneur considering the launch of a new venture, the incubator champions must explore the market potential for their

Ten Steps in the Feasibility Study Process

1. Identify and understand the market.

2. Educate sponsors, community leaders and other stakeholders.

3. Identify obstacles and problems.

4. Create a team of champions.

5. Specify the resources required for successful start-up.

6. Define the requirements and characteristics of the incubator president.

7. Learn from the experiences of other incubators.

8. Develop a written document describing the terms and conditions under which the incubator would be feasible.

9. Ask and answer the critical "to be or not to be" questions.

10. If the decision is made to proceed, get a head start on developing a business plan.

business. Is there a market for an incubator in this community? Identifying and understanding this market is the first and most important step in determining the feasibility of a business incubator. When exploring the market potential, ask these questions:

-   How many start-ups were there last year in this community?
-   What organizations and individuals are serving and supporting them? Are these services working?
-   How can developing new ventures strengthen the community?

By asking questions, potential stakeholders and entrepreneurs are encouraged to consider the idea of a business incubator. If there is a market, this process also can stimulate demand. Talk to:

-   Bankers, lawyers and accountants. They are familiar with start-up companies. How many start-up companies did they interact with last year? Which would they recommend to a business incubator?
-   County commissioners and utility representatives. Describe the concept of a business incubator. Would they provide support?
-   Business leaders of established local companies. Do they have "shelf" technology they want to develop?

- College and university officials. Do they have technology that could be commercialized? Are there graduate students burning with new ideas who want to start companies?
- Angel investors. What business opportunities have they examined? Which ones have they funded?
- Representatives of the local Chamber of Commerce or Small Business Development Center. What services are they already providing to new businesses? What additional services are needed? Are there opportunities for collaboration?
- State agencies that register new business incorporations. How many and what kinds of businesses have started up in the past year? In the past five years?
- Established businesses with potential spin-offs. Would they be interested in the incubator as an off-site "skunk works" or as a source of assistance for new internal ventures?

The exploratory activities related to testing the concept of a business incubator and defining the market also help to stimulate the market and begin the community education process.

In a sense, there are two sets of customers for the incubator, as indicated in Figure 3, "The Incubation Process." The community, through the leadership of the sponsoring institutions, provides start-up resources, ongoing volunteer support and a source of entrepreneurs and entrepreneurial ventures. As a "customer" of the incubator, the community hopes to gain viable ventures that provide job opportunities, an expanded tax base and, sometimes, other derivative benefits, such as neighborhood revitalization.

If the incubator champions can convince community sponsors that the incubator can help companies grow, hence create jobs, then the sponsors should be willing to provide the financial investment necessary to move the incubator from a negative cash flow position during the start-up and ramp-up phases to financial self-sustainability. If the incubator champions cannot garner the support of community sponsors, this may be an indication that the community is not a good market for an incubator. Alternatively, community sponsors may perceive that there is already sufficient infrastructure for the support of new business development and therefore may see an incubator as redundant.

Within this "macro" relationship between the incubator and the community, there is a "micro" relationship between the incubator and the individual incubator company. Each tenant company is a customer for the physical facilities, the shared services and the management assistance programs of the incubator.

By talking with the local Chamber of Commerce, the Small Business Development Center, the business schools in local colleges, angel investors, small business service providers and corporate or university managers responsible for technology commercialization, the champions should be

FIGURE 3

The Incubation Process

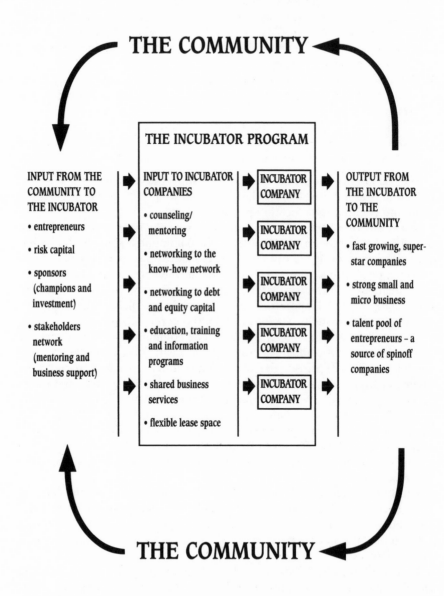

able to size up the market among entrepreneurs for the services an incubator can provide. It also may be appropriate to contact local and state agencies that track filing documents for new businesses.

Except for small communities and incubators that target specific industries or markets, the "supply" of companies is not likely to be a barrier to starting up an incubator. If quality incubator services and resources can be provided at an attractive price, experience suggests that there will be enough candidate companies to enable the incubator to ramp-up to an established business in its own right.

EDUCATE SPONSORS, COMMUNITY LEADERS AND OTHER STAKEHOLDERS

The feasibility study process should stimulate civic and political as well as business leaders to acquire more knowledge about business incubation, to consider "what if" possibilities and to begin the process of managing expectations. A feasibility study must include a substantial component of community education in order to make sure stakeholders understand the "basics" of business incubation. Through the feasibility study, the community and sponsors also gain a shared understanding of the purpose and scope of the incubator, its role in the community and the resources required to launch and sustain the incubator.

It may prove valuable for delegations of community leaders to visit established incubators and to meet with the sponsors who have been involved in incubator feasibility studies in other cities. Attending a trade association meeting, such as a meeting of a state incubator association or the annual conference of the National Business Incubation Association, can provide intensive exposure to the cumulative experience of other incubators. In addition, attending these meetings provides an opportunity to develop relationships with incubator sponsors and stakeholders in communities that have useful experiences to share. Finally, the National Business Incubation Association and other organizations offer training programs that can be cost-effective ways of increasing the sophistication of community leaders, sponsor representatives and other stakeholders.

IDENTIFY OBSTACLES AND PROBLEMS

Getting bright, capable, committed champions involved in the feasibility study process is the best method for generating the creativity and persistence necessary to overcome obstacles. These obstacles include: (1) insufficient financial resources to get through the feasibility study stage and the ramp-up period after the incubator opens; (2) lukewarm support from other community organizations providing business assistance programs that might view the incubator as competition; (3) arguments over the incubator's purpose, with sponsoring institutions each advancing their own agendas, which are not always compatible with each other; (4) pressure from a stakeholder who wants his/her candidate to be appointed incubator president; or (5) a stakeholder who is promoting a particular building which may not be appropriate as the incubator center. A feasibility study, well-defined and executed, provides an opportunity for a rigorous assessment of obstacles and problems and identification of what will be needed to overcome them. This enables sponsors to make decisions based on objective analyses.

CREATE A TEAM OF CHAMPIONS

The number of participants in the feasibility study process is often large. Without leadership, stakeholders are likely to expend their energy and enthusiasm and not get beyond the feasibility study process. Even worse, they may rush through the feasibility study without exercising sufficient due diligence to determine whether the concept will work in their community. The key sponsoring institutions each need to designate a champion. From among the group of champions, someone committed to the development of an incubator needs to step up to the leadership position. Ideally, the lead champion will be in a senior position within his/her organization, will have the clout and the capability to lead the feasibility study effort and will be willing and able to push the decision making process to a conclusion. The champions need to:

- have a sincere and substantial interest in new business development
- be committed to a rational evaluation of whether or not an incubator is a necessary and appropriate vehicle for the support of business start-ups in their community
- exercise determination and persistence in pursuing the process expeditiously and thoroughly

SPECIFY THE RESOURCES REQUIRED
FOR SUCCESSFUL START-UP

The feasibility study may identify a variety of local resources (facilities, equipment, human resources, dollars and in-kind services) that might otherwise not have been available. But beyond reacting to offers of resources from stakeholders, the team of champions needs to determine whether enough of the right kinds of resources will be available. They must make an accurate assessment of the resources that will be needed and determine how they will be acquired—before a commitment to launch the incubator can even be considered. This is an opportunity to begin to characterize the facility or facilities required to accommodate the anticipated mix of client companies and meet the operating objectives of the incubator. Given the objectives of the program and the nature of the envisioned incubator facility, a preliminary analysis of staffing requirements also should be developed.

It is essential to identify the financial resources needed to carry the process through the feasibility study stage and—if the decision is made to proceed—from start-up through ramp-up to self-sustainability. In all three areas—facilities, staffing and finances—it is important to identify the sources of required resources and test the willingness of sponsors to make the necessary commitments.

DEFINE THE REQUIREMENTS AND CHARACTERISTICS OF THE INCUBATOR PRESIDENT

The lead champion and team of champions carry the process forward during the feasibility study stage. If the "to be or not to be" decision is positive, an incubator president must be recruited to assume the mantle of entrepreneurial leadership. The champions need to extend their understanding of the operational dynamics of an incubator to include a definition of the tasks the incubator president must undertake and accomplish. This statement of work can be converted into job specifications for the president and a list of the characteristics of a desirable candidate. Consulting with executive directors and presidents of established incubator programs with a successful track record can be a useful strategy for understanding the desirable characteristics of an incubator president, as well as a way to tap the network for recommendations leading to potential candidates.

LEARN FROM THE EXPERIENCES OF OTHER INCUBATORS

More than 550 incubators have been established in the past 10 years. There are many examples of what works and what does not work regarding selecting a facility, establishing a governance structure, recruiting an incubator president, and so forth. The cumulative experience in the incubator industry demonstrates the importance of a feasibility study in avoiding typical patterns of error.

The experiences of other incubator programs, this book and the wealth of information that the National Business Incubation Association has accumulated should significantly increase the return on investment of time and dollars in the feasibility study process. A properly formulated and executed feasibility study can prevent "classic" incubator errors such as:

- accepting the worst building in town (or if not the worst, then one that simply will not work)
- underestimating the importance of recruiting a competent incubator president to lead the management assistance program
- assuming that an effective management assistance program requires little more than a few referrals to individuals who can assist entrepreneurs in the development of their business plans and a few shared office services

  • failing to define a path to financial self-sustainability
  • failing to manage the incubator like a business

The team of champions may wish to engage a consultant with a proven track record in conducting incubator feasibility studies, developing incubators and/or in managing successful incubator programs to help them make sure they have addressed the critical issues.

DEVELOP A FEASIBILITY DOCUMENT

Most incubator projects are conceived and developed before the governing board is established and the incubator president is identified and recruited. The feasibility study report can provide a valuable record of the early history of the project, enabling the incubator board of directors and staff to have a reference point from which to work and a record of commitments made by the sponsors. Perhaps most important, when the champions commit themselves to a written document, there is a high probability that most of the terms and conditions for feasibility have been identified and are understood. Not all questions will be answered at this stage nor all issues resolved, but the feasibility study document provides a framework within which to organize information, and it establishes the level and types of expectations the champions and stakeholders will have for the incubator.

The incubator champions can reach interim decisions based on best available information. They can also identify and assess areas of uncertainty. The discipline imposed by this process should eventually result in the accumulation of enough positive indicators to permit the champions to reach a go-ahead decision or enough negative indicators to cause them to table the project and avoid a disaster. It will identify the terms and conditions under which the incubator will be feasible.

The specification of resources required for successful start-up will be reflected in financial pro formas developed for the project. At the very least, the sponsors should use these pro formas as a basis for determining whether they are willing to commit to the financial investments required for start-up and ramp-up of the incubator and whether there is a realistic path to self-sustainability.

ADDRESS THE CRITICAL "TO BE OR NOT TO BE" QUESTIONS

By now, it should be clear that the feasibility study process is iterative. In most cases the champions start with limited understanding of business incubators. It is essential to return periodically throughout the process to the critical "to be or not to be" questions and to reassess the answers, based on the accumulation of information and the increasing sophistication of the champions in effectively analyzing that information. Before the final decision is made to proceed or to abandon the concept, revisit and consider these critical questions. These questions are similar to those that any entrepreneur should ask before starting a new business.

Finance

What financial investments and resources will be required for the incubator to be successful? Is there a clear path from start-up to financial self-sustainability? Are the incubator sponsors committed to making the necessary investments and making them in a way that pushes the incubator toward self-sustainability?

Management

Is the team of champions committed to the management/governance process if the project moves ahead? Is the incubator president position fully defined? Is there reasonable confidence that an appropriate president can be recruited?

Market

Is there a market for a business incubator in the community?

Are there enough entrepreneurs to provide a sufficient flow of ventures through the incubator, to satisfy both the cash flow needs of the incubator and the desire of the sponsors for new job-generating companies? Are there enough sponsors willing to provide sufficient investment over whatever period of time is required to establish the incubator as a self-sustainable entity? Are there established programs currently addressing the same needs that the proposed incubator will address? Are these other programs not fulfilling those needs? Will these other programs compete with the incubator for the same market, or will collaboration make all these programs stronger? What value will an incubator add?

The Product or Service

What programs, services and resources will be offered by the incubator to meet the needs of entrepreneurs in the community? How will the incubator's programs and services differ from those offered by other, similar organizations?

The critical questions in these four areas need to be addressed to complete the feasibility study process as a basis for making the "to be or not to be" decision. Then they need to be addressed again when developing the business plan for implementation of the incubator program.

DEVELOP A BUSINESS PLAN

At this stage, the completion of a written feasibility study document signifies the accumulation of sufficient information and understanding to let the sponsors and their champions answer the "to be or not to be" question. Developing a full-blown business plan before hiring the incubator president, who will be responsible for implementation, is not recommended. However, getting a head start on converting the feasibility study document into a business plan can serve as the bridge between "studying" and "starting up" for the team of champions.

After the decision has been made to move ahead and establish an incubator, an appropriate incubator president should be hired as soon as possible. The new president will then be able to play a pivotal role in the further development of the business plan he/she will have to implement. If the team of champions develops the plan before the president is hired, then at least one additional iteration will be required so the president can help shape the plan and facilitate his/her commitment to the implementation of the incubator.

The following steps summarize how to determine incubator feasibility.

ACTION STEPS

FOR DETERMINING INCUBATOR FEASIBILITY

1. Probe the market. Recognize the iterative nature of the feasibility study process. Keep probing the market as information is accumulated and the sophistication of the team of champions increases. This process will generate answers to most of the questions related to the market and to the willingness of sponsors to commit to the financial investments required to proceed. The evidence will accumulate that favors a decision to proceed or a decision to stop.

2. Identify a champion or leader of the team of champions. Ideally, the lead champion is committed to the idea of exploring the feasibility of an incubator and has the capacity to "carry the ball" until a permanent president can be hired. Continue to expand and strengthen the team of champions as long as the process moves forward.

3. Tap external resources to increase the sophistication of the team. Invest in consultants as appropriate. Visit and learn from other incubator programs. Access the information resources and training programs offered by industry trade associations such as National Business Incubation Association.

4. Secure sufficient funding. Institutional sponsor(s) must commit the funding required to complete the feasibility study process and reach the "to be or not to be" decision point. If the decision is made to proceed, secure commitments for the investments required to get from start-up through ramp-up to self-sustainability.

5. Use the written feasibility study to document the process. The feasibility study process will generate a growing information database and will increase the knowledge and sophistication of the sponsors and champions with respect to business incubation.

6. Make the "to be or not to be" decision. At some point the champions must decide that "enough is enough," that they have enough data to make a decision. If the answer is "yes, let's establish an incubator," then begin to develop the business plan and recruit a president.

3

Understanding the Financial Dynamics of Incubators

Understanding the financial dynamics of incubators is critical for achieving self-sustainability. Experience suggests that sponsors often get the numbers wrong, either by being overly optimistic or by making unrealistic assumptions. For example, they often underestimate the length of time and the amount of effort required to grow a new generation of successful companies. To achieve its objectives, the incubator needs to have the resources to grow companies—after the high energy enthusiasm of the incubator launch has faded and before the community is re-energized by incubator companies' successes.

Nothing diminishes the energy and enthusiasm of sponsors, stakeholders and staff more than having to focus month after month, and year after year, on the financial survival of the incubator. If the incubator is going to be around long enough to have an impact, it needs to be self-sustainable. Only then can the sponsors, stakeholders and staff concentrate their energies and capacities on developing incubator client companies, i.e., implementing the First Principle.

BEST PRACTICE #3

STRUCTURE THE INCUBATOR PROGRAM TO BE FINANCIALLY SELF-SUSTAINABLE.

The following framework can be used to understand the financial dynamics of incubators and how to achieve financial self-sustainability.

SOURCES AND USES OF FUNDS

Entrepreneurs who have survived start-up understand that "Cash is king." For an incubator, achieving financial self-sustainability can also be viewed as resolving the cash flow problem. The incubator needs to get

The Financial Dynamics of Incubators

1. Sources and Uses of Funds

2. Subsidy vs. Investment

3. Ramping Up to Self-Sustainability

4. Current vs. Deferred Revenue

5. Paths to Self-Sustainability: Three Models

through the feasibility, start-up/ramp-up stages, when cash flow is typically negative, and achieve break-even. The length of time that sponsors must expect negative cash flow needs to be explicitly stated in the business plan. This time frame will vary, depending on the financial model adopted.

Intelligent and aggressive management of cash flow requires a clear understanding of sources and uses of funds. In current practice, revenue sources and operating costs for most incubators can be grouped as shown in Figure 4, "Sources and Uses of Funds."

Sources of Revenue

Rental Income

For most incubators, rental fees from client companies in the incubator are a primary source of revenue. Hence, making appropriate assumptions about rental income is critical for developing a realistic financial model. The starting point in the analysis should be the following questions.

1. How much space can be rented to companies that would be candidates for location in the incubator?
2. What rental rates can be charged?
3. What percentage of rentable space will be occupied on average once the incubator has ramped up to a relatively steady state with respect to operations?
4. What percentage of rental accounts receivable will be collected?
5. Given answers to questions 2 – 4, how much space needs to be rented in order to satisfy the financial model?

Step 1 of the feasibility study process, "determining the demand for space in the proposed incubator center," answers question #1. Finding enough candidate companies is typically not a problem unless the incubator is to be located in a small rural community. However, attracting high growth potential companies may be a problem until the incubator has a track record.

FIGURE 4

Sources and Uses of Funds

SOURCES OF REVENUE

1. Rental income from companies

2. Fees charged for business services

3. Fees (both current in the form of cash and deferred in the form of royalties and equities) from incubator companies for management assistance

4. Financial support or "investments" from one or more sponsors

COSTS OF OPERATION

1. Real-estate related costs, which may take the form of rent paid to a landlord, or, if the facility is owned by the incubator or its sponsor, costs associated with amortization of debt incurred for acquisition and renovation

2. Costs related to providing shared services

3. Staff salaries

4. Capital expenditures

5. General and administrative costs such as office supplies, marketing materials and professional fees (e.g., for legal and accounting services)

Assuming a sufficient supply of tenants, the questions then become, "How do we rent the space?" e.g., square foot versus unit blocks of space, and "How much do we charge to rent that space?"

KNOW YOUR MARKET

One southwestern incubator, after building a first class facility, discovered that it needed to charge tenants more than $16 per square foot per year to achieve break even. The incubator sponsors estimated that the market would bear between $4 and $5 per square foot. The incubator sponsors did not do an adequate market assessment with their feasibility study and failed to design a workable financial model before constructing their incubator facility. Attracting tenants willing to pay four times the going rental rate was problematic, and expecting sponsors to provide sufficient support indefinitely to cover the differential between the fair market and break-even rental rates was equally unrealistic.

Some people think incubators have to offer entrepreneurs below-market rates, thereby creating artificially low rental rates. Unfortunately, when the subsidies are discontinued, the incubators have to raise the rates and often lose tenants in the process. Rather than being known as "low rent space," incubators need to be positioned as "success environments." Entrepreneurs should be expected to pay market rate rent for space—and even a small premium for flexible leasing terms and for access to all elements of this "success environment."

NBIA statistics suggest that most incubators reach 75% occupancy within three years. However, incubators that commit to an aggressive marketing effort and are diligent about adopting best practices may reach full occupancy in less than three years and maintain average occupancy rates in excess of 90%. On the other hand, incubators with poor marketing programs that do not deliver value to their customers often find themselves with half-empty buildings and a chronic cash flow problem.

Collection Rate

No matter how conscientious an incubator staff is about making collections, it is unreasonable to expect a 100% collection rate of rent. Most incubator companies are start-ups with a high degree of financial risk and uncertainty. They are, by definition, risky tenants. But with an aggressive and professional approach to collections, it is reasonable to collect 90% to 95% of receivables.

Size of Incubator

For incubators that plan to be self-sustainable based on current revenues, 30,000 to 40,000 square feet of rentable space is the minimum required to support financial self-sustainability. The only condition under which a smaller incubator is feasible is a long-term commitment of a sponsor to continuing the investment in the incubator as a vehicle for economic development, fostering community relations, technology commercialization or some related goal. With a sponsor underwriting some of the costs of the incubator, less of the total revenue needs to be derived from rental income; hence less space is required to achieve sustainability.

The size of the incubator also depends on the amount of space that must be rented to achieve the financial model that is adopted in the incubator business plan. Use the following simple formula to make a preliminary estimate.

Revenue from Rents Projected by the Model

Average Rental Rate	x	Average Occupancy Rate	x	Average Collection Rate	=	Total Amou. of Rental Spa. Required for the Model

For example, assume:

1. The average rental rate will be $8 per square foot.
2. The occupancy rate is pegged at 75%.
3. The collection rate will average 95%.
4. The financial model requires that the contribution from rents to total revenues must be $228,000.

Using the formula noted above,

$$\frac{\$228,000}{\$8 \,/\, \text{square foot} \ \ x \ .75 \ x \ .95} \ = \ 40,000 \text{ square feet}$$

In this example, the incubator facility would need to have at least 40,000 square feet of rentable space to generate the rental income specified in its business plan.

Fees for Shared Services

Incubators typically offer one or more of the following shared business services:

- receptionist
- telephone answering
- word processing
- bookkeeping
- copier and fax services
- access to a conference room

The costs associated with delivering shared services can be a significant part of the total expenditures of an incubator program. With careful pricing, marketing, and management of shared services (especially billing and collections), excess revenues can be generated that can be used to help defray other program costs. Client companies will usually be willing to pay a premium rate for the convenience of using a copier, fax machine, or telephone system, especially if they can avoid capital expenditures. The incubator can provide these services at rates that will generate revenues which exceed the cost.

Revenue from Management Assistance Programs

Current Revenue. Some incubators charge a separate fee for the management assistance they provide. In other incubators, a sponsor may underwrite some or all of the costs of management assistance as a line item in their economic development budget. Still other incubators bundle management assistance into a package rate that includes leased space, use of some common spaces and some shared services.

Access to management assistance is a benefit of the incubator and is used as a "carrot" in many incubators' marketing programs. Some incubators have "productized" these services, offer them for a fee and/or require additional compensation in the form of royalties or equity participation.

THE "TASTER" PROGRAM

One incubator network has structured its assistance program into five service tracks:
- Office Practice
- Business Planning
- Financial Management
- Marketing and Sales
- Legal Assistance

Client companies are introduced to each service track through a one- or two-hour "taster" program, which includes a well-defined deliverable to the company and an introduction to the second step in the track. Each one of the first steps in all five tracks is given a title that identifies the "taster" as a stand-alone service product (e.g., The Six Hats Method of Business Plan Development; The S.C.O.R.E. card and Template Program for Developing Your Marketing Strategy; A Forty Point Legal Audit of Your Business). Each track has an average of eight steps, and each step has a clearly defined deliverable and a required commitment, in time and cost, that the client company must make. Each service track provides a clear path for increasing the sophistication and capacity of the participating entrepreneurs.

The incubator president credits the program with (1) helping client companies link up with experts in the "know-how network," (2) generating revenue for the incubator, (3) stimulating client referrals and (4) identifying the incubator as a service provider to entrepreneurs in the community.

Deferred Revenue. Recognizing that start-up companies are seldom able to pay for all the services they need, some incubators require companies to pay current fees and also share a small percentage of their stock or their future licensing/royalty revenue stream—a form of deferred compensation for services being provided before a company can pay for them.

BOARD FOR HIRE

One incubator created a program to provide the equivalent of a "board of directors for hire," to serve the board oversight function until incubator companies were ready to form a board of their own. Of the dozen or so companies that have participated so far, one is now on the verge of a public financing through which the incubator expects to harvest about $35,000.

A few words of caution are appropriate at this juncture. One of the risks of providing management assistance in return for cash is related to the incubator's own need for cash. The pressure to generate new revenues may lead the incubator director to target the services to those tenants who can afford to pay and not provide as much assistance to those who cannot pay. This approach may facilitate achieving the Second Principle: *manage the incubator as a business* but may diminish the incubator's capacity to provide assistance to high potential companies who cannot afford to pay for services at a time when they need them the most. The First Principle is paramount: *The incubator's mission is to grow companies*, and therefore focusing assistance on those companies with the highest growth potential should be the priority.

With respect to equity and royalty agreements, the probability of return is usually low, and the time to harvest is typically long. The incubator business plan should identify and require the amount of investment that needs to be made over the long haul to permit program continuity until the "winners" emerge and royalties or equity can be converted to cash. Some incubators may elect to exclude potential equity/royalty revenues from their plan for achieving financial sustainability and treat them as a "windfall"—if and when they happen.

Sponsor Investment

Sponsors should expect to make a financial investment during the incubator's feasibility, start-up and ramp-up stages. This investment bridges the gap between revenues and expenses in these early stages, allowing the incubator the time necessary to develop a stream of revenues to cover its operating costs. For most incubators, sponsors and management should develop and commit to a plan that leads to financial self-sustainability. After achieving this mode of operation, the incubator will no longer require sponsor investment. However, this does not preclude the possibility that in some cases sponsors may choose to make additional or ongoing investments to further enhance the capacity of the incubator to support the growth of companies that create jobs.

Sponsor investments do not always come in the form of cash. Non-cash investments can often create a framework within which the incubator, whose customers are high risk, start-up ventures, can structure itself to operate like a business. For example, if loaned executives and volunteers from the sponsors can augment the incubator staff and take responsibility for some of the operational tasks, the incubator staff is freed to focus on helping incubator companies. Alternatively, sponsors that locate one of their own operational groups in the incubator can become anchor tenants and provide a reliable source of rental income to the incubator. In addition, sponsors can often provide access to people, equipment and services at a reduced rate to the incubator and/or its companies. The overall effect of these non-cash "investments" is to increase revenues or decrease operating costs—thereby diminishing the incubator's need for cash.

Costs of Operation

Real Estate-Related Costs

For most incubators, creativity in dealing with the real estate-related issues is the key to achieving financial self-sustainability. For those that succeed, the surplus of real estate-related revenues over real estate-related costs is one way to fund the management assistance program.

A significant percentage of entrepreneurs who are attracted to an incubator and who have high promise for growing successful entrepreneurial companies will view lease space as a necessity and will be willing to pay fair market rates plus a small premium for that space. The willingness to trade the guest bedroom or garage for incubator space is enhanced when payments for "space" also provide access to the other programs, resources and expertise offered through the incubator.

As noted in the discussion about sponsor investments, it is common for the real estate deal to be structured so that the incubator does not bear the full cost. For example, one of the sponsors may own an underutilized building and may be willing to "loan" the building to the incubator program. The sponsor may charge the incubator program little or no rent and instead gain benefit in other ways, e.g., (1) "goodwill" generated by their "donation," (2) the creation of a channel for technology transfer, (3) a living laboratory for the study of entrepreneurship, (4) a tax advantage related to the donation, or (5) the creation of a market for their own services or products. Alternatively sponsors may choose to direct their cash investment in the incubator to the acquisition of the facility, thereby enabling the incubator to generate revenue that, if managed correctly, could provide the basis for financial self-sustainability and obviate the need for further cash investments. The opportunity to structure this kind of creative real estate deal is one of the key criteria for judging the attractiveness of a prospective incubator facility (see Chapter 7).

Facilities Operations and Maintenance Costs

Typical costs in this category include:

- ongoing build-out or facility conversion
- building repairs and maintenance
- cleaning
- security
- maintenance of landscaping and parking
- utilities (telecom and HVAC)
- property and other taxes
- insurance

Usually the incubator is expected to bear the full costs of operating and maintaining the facility. Fully assessing these costs is another critical issue to consider before acquiring an appropriate facility, an issue that is often not adequately addressed.

Capital Expenditures

Although the sponsors may be able to structure an attractive real estate deal, the incubator will be expected to bear most or all of the costs related to additional capital expenditures, such as major renovations or installation of new utilities. Also included in this category are the costs of purchasing business equipment, furnishings and fixtures, such as:

- telephone systems
- copier
- fax machine
- computers
- furnishings for the administrative offices, conference room and the company offices

Incubator champions often seek donations from sponsors and their companies for some or all of these items.

Costs Related to Providing Shared Services

The capital costs related to providing shared services (e.g., acquiring communications, computing, and copying equipment) were noted above. The incubator may also pay sponsors or other institutions for access to facilities and resources (e.g., laboratories, equipment, libraries, shops, parts stores, etc.), as well as those who provide services such as bookkeeping. Usually these costs are simply passed through to the incubator tenants who use the services, often with some markup to cover administrative costs.

Incubators sometimes underestimate the difficulties and the costs of collecting the accounts receivable related to shared services in a timely fashion. This can be especially difficult for an incubator that is embedded within a sponsor institution.

THE IMPORTANCE OF TIMELY COLLECTIONS

One incubator company shipped its first product, a new software package with diskettes and manuals, under an account established through the mailroom of the incubator's institutional sponsor, shortly before graduating from the incubator and moving out of the area. Because of the slow rate at which paperwork moved through the institutional bureaucracy, the $700 shipping bill did not appear on the desk of the incubator president until two months after the company left the area. The company acknowledged the debt and agreed in writing that it would pay when cash flow turned positive. However, the company was recently acquired, and its new parent is ignoring the obligation.

Even though shared business services are highly valued by many incubator companies, they can be time-consuming to administer, their use can be difficult to track, and collections of charges can sometimes be a challenge.

General and Administrative (G&A) Costs

Like any other business, an incubator will have general and administrative expenses, including those related to office supplies, marketing materials, professional fees (e.g., for legal and accounting services), telephone usage, mail, shipping and staff training. Some of these costs can be absorbed by sponsors, especially if the incubator is embedded within a parent or sponsoring organization.

SPONSOR SUPPORT FOR G & A

For one embedded incubator, accounting and annual audits are provided by the central administration. Similarly, the sponsor has established an account with a local law firm for all legal services, and the incubator is not required to pay directly for these services.

While the incubator manager needs to be aggressive at controlling G&A costs, he/she must look for opportunities to invest G&A dollars in improving staff productivity. Given the pivotal role the staff plays in delivering business assistance, this is an area where a modest investment can have a big payoff in terms of productivity.

One of the primary functions of an incubator is to serve as an intermediary between expertise and resources and the incubator companies that can benefit from them. There are G&A costs associated with playing the intermediary role. The incubator must invest in developing the network of individuals and institutions that can provide this expertise and these resources. That means spending G&A funds on communications media—mail, fax, electronic mail, telephone—and even, when necessary, on travel for face-to-face meetings with potential providers of resources. In addition, incubators should join NBIA and send a representative to the annual NBIA conference to gain valuable information about the industry and learn about new developments and solutions to common problems.

The incubator budget needs to accommodate the costs related to achieving and sustaining best practices. It is usually most cost effective to utilize the experiences of others to efficiently resolve problems, meet challenges, and implement new solutions. The incubator staff, sponsors and stakeholders should take advantage of opportunities to participate in state and national associations, such as NBIA, and the incubator budget needs to include costs associated with this participation, visits to "best practices" incubators and an occasional consultant who can help determine where the incubator needs help.

Staff Salaries

For many incubators, staff salaries represent one half or more of the total incubator budget. Staff dedication to delivering business assistance to the incubator companies differentiates an incubator from a real estate project targeting start-up companies. To obtain the services of a competent, full time incubator president, the incubator needs to include in its budget somewhere between $50,000 and $100,000 plus appropriate fringe benefits, depending on the local market. A dynamic incubator, occupying the minimal space recommended here, i.e., 30,000 to 40,000 square feet of rentable space, will also require the services of a secretary or receptionist and a business operations manager. Assuming that none of this staffing capacity is provided pro bono by sponsors, the incubator will need to include in its budget an additional $50,000 to $60,000 plus fringe benefits for the receptionist and the business operations manager. These costs are likely to be higher in areas with a high cost of living and may be lower in others.

A best practices incubator will be structured to take into account the two competing demands: (1) the need to achieve long-term financial self-sustainability, and (2) the need to provide appropriate staffing to manage the business operations of the incubator and to provide the business assistance that helps entrepreneurs grow their companies. The tension between these two demands is manageable when viewed in the context of the three basic principles of successful incubation: focus on growing companies, manage the incubator like a successful company, and provide differentiated programs of business assistance.

SUBSIDY VS. INVESTMENT

Sponsors often provide infusions of cash in order to sustain incubator operations. But if the cash is treated as a "subsidy," it creates a fundamentally different relationship between the sponsors and the incubator than if it is treated as a "public investment." The term "investment" implies that a business judgment has been made and that there is a reasonable expectation of a return on that investment. An investment represents a challenge to the recipient to succeed and to provide a return to the investor. "Subsidy" refers to a grant, usually made by a government entity, to an enterprise that is perceived as having benefit to the public, but which needs cash to "subsist," or survive. It suggests a dependency relationship. Best practices incubators develop investment, not dependent, relationships with their sponsors.

Unfortunately some incubators start with unrealistic expectations, fundamental confusion about the nature of new business creation and development and inadequate business plans. In this situation, there is no understanding or agreement about the cash infusions sponsors must make if the incubator is going to reach self-sustainability. Many sponsors have been led to believe that somehow—almost magically—the incubator will be the catalyst for stimulating an instantaneous turnaround of the local economy.

When the incubator falls short of expectations, operates marginally from a financial perspective and requires a continuing infusion of cash just to stay afloat, sponsors begin to view their cash contributions as a "subsidy" rather than as an "investment." The process of sustaining that subsidy becomes a tremendous drain on the time, energy, and enthusiasm of the incubator president, the board, the financial sponsors and even the incubator companies. The mad scramble for funding detracts from the mission of the incubator: growing companies.

In a best practices incubator, the business plan represents an agreement between the sponsors, the board and the incubator management. If the plan reflects realistic expectations regarding performance, and if all the participants fulfill their obligations, then the incubator is likely to succeed. The operational performance of a best practices incubator should meet or exceed plan. Any continuing financial support reflects the commitments made during the planning process as a *quid pro quo* for successful operation. It is much healthier to view the financial contributions of the sponsors as investments aimed at achieving company growth, job creation and eventual economic development rather than as subsidies for the incubator.

RAMPING UP TO SELF-SUSTAINABILITY

Some concepts are easy to understand and difficult to implement. Ramping up to self-sustainability is one of those concepts. During the feasibility, start-up and ramp-up stages, the incubator project will operate in a negative cash flow situation, and sponsors will need to invest resources. If the program is well designed and implemented, the time will come when the incubator should be able to operate in a self-sustainable mode. When the program is not well designed and implemented, the sponsors may find themselves with an unhappy choice: subsidize the incubator indefinitely or shut it down.

As noted earlier, sponsors must take the lead in raising the funds necessary for the feasibility study phase and for supporting incubator operations during start-up and ramp-up. Sponsors may also recruit other business leaders, politicians, organizational leaders, ministers and others who are identified as community leaders. These individuals can work closely with sponsors to develop funding strategies that will serve the incubator and client companies long term. In addition, community leaders may have personal and institutional networks that could be sources of funding or other resources and political support. As always, the benefits of involving these individuals must be weighed against the costs of recruiting, sustaining and managing them.

In addition to providing their own institutional funds, sponsors may pursue funding from other local, state, and regional agencies that are willing to support incubator development as part of an overall economic development strategy. These include:

1. *State and local economic development agencies,* which are typically involved in bringing jobs into their states and in working with under-

developed communities with high unemployment.

2. *Local banks*, which may be sponsors and participate in incubator development because incubators create potential business relationships for the banks. In addition in some cases, banks may be able to satisfy community service goals by participating in incubator development.

3. The local *Chamber of Commerce* may be a sponsor of an incubator within its traditional role as an advocate of small businesses.

4. Public *colleges, universities and community colleges* may see incubators as a way to fulfill their mandates to provide their communities with technical assistance, research and training in new technology.

5. *Churches,* in some communities, are activists in neighborhood development. An incubator can be a source of jobs for the parishioners of a church, which in turn provides the basis for a safer community, crime reduction and property ownership by neighborhood residents.

6. *Corporate foundations and community foundations* are sometimes willing to support incubators that work with and educate entrepreneurs and small companies.

7. *Federal agencies* that have been involved in funding incubator development:
   - U.S. Department of Commerce, through the Economic Development Administration
   - Department of Housing and Urban Development, through the Community Development Block Grant funds
   - Department of Health and Human Services, through its discretionary funds
   - Department of Agriculture, through the Rural Electrification Administration's Rural Economic Development Loan and Grant Program and through the Farmer's Home Administration
   - The Tennessee Valley Authority
   - The Appalachian Regional Commission

How long will it take and how much investment will be required? Under reasonable conditions and with good planning and execution, past experience suggests that sponsors should plan on a three- to five-year ramp-up period. The investment required will depend on the size of the facility, the number of parties-at-interest and the amount of money each party is willing to contribute or "invest."

CURRENT VS. DEFERRED REVENUE

The financial plan needs to be structured so that after the ramp-up stage the incubator can be self-sustaining. However, the long-term financial strategy may also include a deferred revenue stream. The eventual payoff of an equity or a deferred royalty agreement with highly successful incubator companies can substantially enhance the long-term viability of the incubator program and can be the basis for expanding the business assistance program, while still maintaining a balanced budget. Deferred revenue may be treated as an "endowment" which over time may be sufficient to replace sponsor "investments."

For most incubators, the financial plan should be structured so that financial self-sustainability can be achieved after the ramp-up stage, based on current revenues alone. However, there are two compelling reasons why the incubator's long-term financial strategy should include deferred revenues.

First, the process of negotiating a deferred fee arrangement causes both the incubator management and the client companies to recognize that the incubator and the community are making an investment in the companies at a point in time. While there may be a difference of opinion concerning how to value that investment, there can be no doubt that such an investment is being made. Sponsors invest in incubator programs through a variety of mechanisms: (1) investment of cash during start-up and ramp-up to achieve a balanced budget; (2) allocation of facilities and resources at less than full cost; and/or (3) the commitment of time by volunteer support personnel. The investment is made with the conviction that incubators improve the odds that new companies will survive, grow and become successful. The incubator provides valuable services at a time when participating companies are least able to pay for those services, thereby creating a dilemma for the incubator and its sponsors, i.e., how to provide the services needed with less than full cost reimbursement.

The sponsors may choose to "write off" the investment in return for the benefits to the community and thus provide a community service. Alternatively the incubator may structure the relationship with its companies to provide mechanisms for collecting both current and deferred fees. Typically the deferred fees will be generated through royalty and/or equity agreements between the incubator and its companies.

Dealing with all the issues related to deferred fees can be a reality check for both the incubator management team and the incubator company entrepreneurs. This process will encourage the incubator president to be selective and aggressive about the investment of limited resources and the incubator company entrepreneurs to be attentive to maximizing the value of the incubator in the development of their companies, since they are explicitly paying for the assistance.

Second, incentive compensation tied to deferred revenue can be a significant part of the total compensation package of the incubator president. Given the demanding workload of most incubator presidents and the modest salaries most incubators provide, top-performing incubator presidents are often lured away to better paying positions. Encouraging incubator presidents to maintain their commitment over the long haul in order to participate in the harvest of equity/royalty positions may be the best strategy sponsors can adopt for retaining the talents of a top-performing president.

WARNING: For most incubators in most communities, the feasibility of achieving significant returns from equity and/or deferred royalty positions is low and the time to harvest is long. Consequently, the financial viability of the incubator should not depend on deferred revenues. Sponsors should not expect to retain a talented incubator president with a low salary and the promise of long-term potential payoff. Instead, deferred revenues should be an incremental addition to an appropriate and attractive current compensation package.

PATHS TO SELF-SUSTAINABILITY: THREE MODELS

The experiences of actual incubators whose operations have evolved over time suggests three models that lead to financial self-sustainability. Real estate operations, sponsor investments, and the harvest of equity are the dominant sources of revenue which fuel the models.

Paths to Financial Self-Sustainability

The Real Estate Model

The Real Estate Plus Sponsor Investment Model

The Venture Capital Model

The Real Estate Model

In the real estate model, financial support is a front-end investment to cover the launch and ramp-up of the incubator until revenues are sufficient to cover the costs of the core program. The business plan of the incubator assumes no further financial support from the sponsors once self-sustainability is achieved. Of course, in subsequent years, the incubator president may decide to develop and implement additional programs or services beyond those defined in the business plan, and he/she may approach the sponsors for additional funds and support. The Financial Statement of a Real Estate Model Incubator is shown in Figure 5.

A UNIVERSITY-RELATED INCUBATOR

The incubator is embedded within a university rather than operating as a separate, independent not-for-profit corporation. The university has established an operating agreement that allows the incubator program to operate on a financially self-sustainable basis as long as the program is well-managed. The university requires no rent payments from the incubator but does require the incubator to cover the costs of retiring

the renovation debt out of its operations. Historically this has amount-
ed to about 20% of the operating revenues. The incubator also benefits
from its host institution by receiving some of the standard services provided to all university departments, e.g., legal, accounting and insurance
services, at no charge.

In return the university enjoys a number of benefits including:
- substantial public relations value from its support of regional economic development
- a magnet for donations from entrepreneurial alumni who are excit-
  ed about the program
- the opportunity to bring real world entrepreneurship into the academic experience of its students and faculty
- a mechanism to promote technology transfer

The university and the incubator are both satisfied with the benefits
each gains from the symbiotic relationship; the benefits to each outweigh the costs. Under this arrangement, the incubator has been operated like a business on a break-even basis as a department of the parent
institution since its inception. The building is large enough and the typical occupancy rate is high enough to generate sufficient revenues to
cover all operating costs, including the salary of the incubator president.
The shared services program is designed so that revenues cover costs.
Most importantly, the nature of the operating agreement eliminates any
requirement that the incubator justify and continually fight for the
financial support of its sponsor. As long as it meets operating expectations, the incubator receives this support. A summary financial statement for the actual operation of this incubator during fiscal year 1993 is
provided in Figure 5.

Although the 1993 financial statement records zero income from
deferred revenues, this incubator has incorporated deferred revenues in
its long-term financial plan. The incubator maintains a reserve account
on its balance sheet, which is designed to provide funds for non-routine
expenses that are not part of its normal operating budget. These non-
routine expenses include major improvements to the facility and capital
expenditures for equipment. Although the 1993 operating statement
includes ongoing payments related to renovation debt retirement, the
balloon payments on the two renovation bonds will be made from this
reserve account. So far, two deferred revenue payments from the sale of
stock in two incubator companies have added approximately $60,000 to
the reserve account. The incubator retains equity positions in approximately twenty additional incubator companies and expects the harvest
of these positions to be sufficient to cover the final renovation bond balloon payment of $200,000 in 1996.

FIGURE 5

Summary 1993 Financial Statement for Incubator Operating Under the Real Estate Model

Income

Rent	$273,000[1]
Reimbursable Services	86,000
Contract with Sponsor(s)	0
Sponsor Investment	0
Deferred Revenues	0
Total Income	**$359,000**

Expenses

Salaries and Benefits	$108,000[2]
Renovation Debt Service	57,000[3]
Utilities	36,000
Facilities Maintenance	22,000
Property Taxes	19,000
Equipment and Supplies	10,000
Telephone	5,000
Travel	4,000
Miscellaneous	12,000
Reimbursable Services	86,000
Total Expenses	**$359,000**

NOTES:

(1) Rent: This incubator operates out of three buildings with total leasable space of about 40,000 square feet. Two of the three buildings are 100% occupied; the third facility, which was recently acquired, is still in ramp-up mode. Thirty-five thousand square feet are currently leased at an average annual rate of $8/square foot, which is approximately fair market.

Anchor tenants occupy about 10,000 square feet and include one other business assistance program with federal and state funding, two university departments and three established companies. The remainder of the space is occupied by thirty companies, ranging from a one-person service firm in a 150 square foot office to a twelve-person R&D firm in 2,000 square feet of laboratory space.

(2) Salaries and Benefits: The incubator staff is composed of a full-time president, who is paid between $60,000 and $70,000 annually; a full-time receptionist; and a part-time business manager.

(3) Renovation Debt Service: A moth-balled classroom/office building was renovated by the university as an incubator with a $600,000 Indus-

trial Development Authority bond and a $200,000 bond issued by a state urban development agency. The financial model of this incubator calls for the first bond to be serviced and retired with current revenues. The second bond has a substantial balloon payment due 15 years after the start-up of the incubator. The harvest of equity positions in one or more incubator companies is expected to cover the balloon payment.

The Real Estate Plus Sponsor Investment Model

The Real Estate Plus Sponsor Investment Model is a variation of the first model. Revenues from the operation of the incubator facility and shared services are augmented by ongoing sponsor investments, which enable the incubator to cover operating costs. The sponsors may have a charter to deliver business assistance to incubator companies which can be discharged through the incubator. When the incubator provides a service which directly benefits the sponsors, they are often willing to underwrite the costs of these services under a defined service agreement.

This "investment" enables an incubator facility to (1) operate in less than 30,000 square feet, (2) be less dependent on anchor tenants as a source of steady cash flow and (3) be more selective in accepting high growth potential incubator companies. Figure 6 displays the budget of an incubator operating under this model.

A GOVERNMENT-RELATED INCUBATOR

The incubator currently occupies a single facility with approximately 16,000 square feet of net leasable space, of which about 75% is leased. However, it is in the process of expanding into a new and larger facility, which will have total net leasable space of about 30,000 square feet.

As the cash flow statement indicates in Figure 6, the budget is designed for break-even. About one-third of the operating expenses are covered by revenues generated from rental of space and other tenant income. The remaining two-thirds of the expenses are covered through sponsor investments and a contract with the city to provide management assistance to new ventures.

Once the new facility is operational and fully leased, the incubator board projects that the 70% of the operating costs will be covered by revenues from operations. The costs of the business assistance program are underwritten by a contract for services with the city and through other sponsor support. The board considers the incubator part of the overall regional economic development strategy, believes it deserves public and private financial investments and argues that the "return on investment" is companies that grow faster and add jobs more quickly than if there had been no incubator.

The president has indicated that, as the build-out of the new facility is completed and occupancy increases, the incubator will move closer to the real estate financial model. However, the board and sponsors are committed to continue to provide investment through a contract for services.

The board and the management of this incubator have decided at this stage that the administrative costs of implementing an equity-based deferred revenue program with their client companies outweigh the long-term return on investment from harvesting equity positions. Instead the incubator president has implemented a loan program that carries a relatively high interest rate commensurate with the increased risk of providing debt financing to early-stage companies with limited assets. In addition several graduate companies have provided donations to the incubator in recognition of the value of the incubator's assistance in the development of their firms. The sponsors view the jobs created by the incubator firms as the primary return on the investment to the community by the incubator.

FIGURE 6

Summary 1993-94 Cash Flow Budget for Case Incubator Operating Under the Real Estate Plus Sponsor Investment Model

Income
Rent $79,000 [1]
Reimbursable Services   40,000
Contract with Sponsor(s)   157,000
Sponsor Investment   52,000
Deferred Revenues   0
Total Income $328,000

Expenses
Salaries and Benefits $160,000 [2]
Renovation Debt Service   0
Utilities   34,000
Facilities Maintenance   19,000
Property Taxes   0
Equipment and Supplies   9,000
Telephone   26,000
Travel   4,000
Miscellaneous   76,000 [3]
Reimbursable Services   0
Total Expenses $328,000

NOTES:

(1) Rent: During the budget year reflected in the preceding figure, this incubator was in transition. During part of the year it was still operating out of its demonstration site with 12,000 s.f. of total leased space and eight participating companies, two in light manufacturing and six service companies. In the latter part of the fiscal year, the incubator moved to a new facility with 30,000 s.f. of available space and began ramping up. The incubator continues to have a mix of service and light manufacturing companies, and has retained two of its early successful graduates as anchor tenants in the new facility.

(2) Salaries and Benefits: The incubator is staffed with a president, an operations manager, a full-time office manager and a part-time receptionist. The compensation packages for the staff of this incubator are comparable to those of the first model.

(3) Miscellaneous: The budget of this incubator carries no costs associated with the acquisition or initial renovation of the incubator. However, in comparison with the incubator in the first model, it must carry the costs of insurance and security, which amount to about one-third of the miscellaneous line item. Almost half of the miscellaneous line item is dedicated to capital expenditures and a reserve for build-out of the facility.

WARNING: Sponsor willingness to "invest" in an incubator may vary with elections, changes in personnel and changes in the economic fortunes of cities, counties, or sponsor companies. Most incubator presidents and sponsors argue that the management assistance provided by a business incubator is a low cost way of stimulating the development of new businesses that generate jobs. But given the significant competition in most communities for the shrinking economic development dollar, sponsors are by no means an assured source of revenue. In addition, there is a cost of sustaining the contributions from the sponsors: the time the president spends maintaining relationships with sponsors—which is time *not* spent working with companies. Fighting for an annual cash infusion from sponsors to sustain the incubator program can become a political battle, which in turn can become a major distraction from the mission of the incubator.

THE IMPORTANCE OF A CHAMPION

An eastern university incubator started up with the university president and the director of the university's research foundation as champions. Both individuals died within six months of the start-up of the incubator, leaving it without a champion. The university official who was subsequently assigned responsibility for the incubator program was only concerned with minimizing university exposure and focused his efforts on trying to abrogate the lease. In addition, without the political clout of its high level champions, the financial support provided to the incubator by a state economic development agency was significantly reduced. Although the incubator has so far survived, both the incubator president and the entrepreneurs report that the impact of the incubator has been diminished.

The Venture Capital Model

Although deferred revenues from equity/royalty positions in incubator companies should be considered in the financial model of any incubator, very few communities currently have the capacity to support a pure venture capital financial model. "Capacity" is defined as sufficient current or future firms with the potential to produce a venture capital-like return on investment. Indicators of capacity include (1) the presence of an active angel or seed capital network with enough history to record a few successes; (2) an entrepreneurial community in which several ventures have grown from start-up to $50 million or more in annual revenues during the past decade; and (3) a sufficiently large community of entrepreneurial ventures to generate an annual flow of five to ten high potential start-ups into the incubator for at least ten years. However, based on the experience of the venture capital industry, perhaps only one in 50, or even one in 100, high growth potential firms admitted to an incubator will achieve a venture capital-like return on investment at "harvest," which almost always entails acquisition or initial public offering (IPO) as exit strategies.

For those communities with the capacity to support the venture capital model, the sponsors may choose to view the incubator as a vehicle for seed capital investment. In this situation, the dynamics of the venture capital industry are likely to influence the incubator's financial structure. Taken to the extreme, the incubator would recruit and only admit companies with the potential for venture capital-like returns on investment. The sponsors should expect to invest for a minimum of ten to fifteen years in exchange for the potential of a substantial "hit" when one or more of the participating companies succeed. Such a windfall should produce enough cash, which, if invested wisely, should eliminate the need for further financial support from the sponsors.

Because the incubator in this model (see Figure 7) focuses on companies with high growth potential, it does not accept other companies, such as anchor tenants, solely for the purpose of providing real estate revenue. The amount of space required for this kind of incubation will be less than in the other models because the sponsors are willing to accept a tradeoff. In order to focus exclusively on high potential companies and to eliminate distractions related to non-high growth companies, the sponsors commit to long-term financial support and are willing to have the incubator operate in a negative cash flow situation while they await the harvest of one or more of the equity or royalty positions in client companies.

Although a few incubator programs and innovation centers in the United States are attempting to implement this model or variations of it, there is not yet enough experience to verify the underlying assumptions. Therefore, it is very important to understand those assumptions. Sponsors should continue to test the assumptions, evaluate the model, and adjust their implementation strategies as experience dictates.

FIGURE 7

Summary Annual Financial Statement for Incubator Operating Under the Venture Capital Model

(Prior to Harvest of Equity or Royalty Positions)

Income	
Rent	$73,000 [1] [3]
Reimbursable Services	86,000
Contract with Sponsor(s)	0
Sponsor Investment	200,000
Deferred Revenues	0
Total Income	**$359,000**

Expenses	
Salaries and Benefits	$108,000 [2] [3]
Renovation Debt Service	57,000
Utilities	36,000
Facilities Maintenance	22,000
Property Taxes	19,000
Equipment and Supplies	10,000
Telephone	5,000
Travel	4,000
Miscellaneous	12,000
Reimbursable Services	86,000
Total Expenses	**$359,000**

Net Income	**0**

NOTES:
(1) Revenues (excluding deferred revenues related to royalty and equity positions): Assume that at steady state the incubator will serve ten companies which occupy and pay for 10,000 square feet of incubator space. The average annual rental rate in current dollars is pegged at $7.30 per square foot. Assume five new companies enter the incubator each year and five graduate, i.e., that there is a rapid throughput of companies— "up or out" after two years. Also assume that compensation to the incubator for management assistance provided to client companies takes the form of equity or royalty positions, which may eventually be

converted to deferred revenue. In the short term the sponsors invest to cover the short-fall.

(2) Costs: The model has the same cost structure as the real estate model displayed in Figure 5.

(3) Inflation rate: Assume that costs and revenues will escalate at comparable rates. (All numbers are in current dollars.) Hence, sponsor investment must increase at the rate of inflation each year, until harvest. For example, if the inflation rate is 5% annually, the sponsor investment will have to increase 5% each year, i.e., from $200,000 in year 1 to $310,265 in year 10.

If the following objectives could be achieved, the incubator would become financially self-sufficient in year 11:

Hit Rate: One out of 50 incubator companies achieves a venture capital-type success within the ten years.

Harvest: It is assumed that the incubator will have a residual 5% interest in the "big hit" company after whatever rounds of financing have been required to get the company to the point of harvest and that by year 10, the company has a market value of $50 million in current dollars. The 5% residual equity position held by the incubator can then be converted into $2.5 million in cash. If the $2.5 million is placed into an investment account and the investment account yields 5% annually after inflation, the incubator will receive $125,000 annually to support operations thereafter. The remaining companies must perform well enough as a group to generate a royalty and equity cash flow equivalent to $75,000 in current dollars.

Achieving these objectives would mean that total revenue from the investment account plus equity and royalty positions in year 11 would equal $200,000 in current dollars, i.e., enough to make the incubator financially self-sufficient. Other combinations of outcomes may produce similar levels of deferred revenues. It may also be possible to reduce sponsor investment sooner, depending on whether the equity and royalty agreements with the incubator companies begin producing income before year 10. On the other hand, the companies may underperform with respect to these objectives, hence continuing sponsor investment may be required beyond year 10 in order to sustain incubator operations.

There are several major challenges in making the venture capital model work. The biggest challenge is recruiting enough high potential ventures. In addition, the typical sponsors of incubators have little or no experience with venture capital investing, and may find it difficult to sustain the ongoing financial investment required during the first ten years or more to get to the point of payoff.

Without the involvement of venture capital professionals, the payoff may never come. Alternatively, venture capitalists may simply allow the sponsors and the incubator management to do the early stage high risk investing, then come along later and "cherry pick" the best deals or squeeze the

equity position of the seed investors in return for whatever larger investment may be required to get to the harvest. As noted earlier, few communities have enough high potential companies to make it feasible for them to
adopt this strategy from the outset.

Clearly, the three financial models described in this chapter are not
mutually exclusive. A best-practices incubator may be able to find a way to
operate without the ongoing financial support of sponsors, while still taking
advantage of opportunities to acquire equity or royalty positions in its
client companies in exchange for business assistance. It is important to recognize that any number of potential changes can drastically affect the operation of the incubator, including changes within the sponsoring institutions, a change of incubator directors, or a change of facilities. Still, given
the long time horizon that is required for the development of a generation
of new ventures, the commitments of the sponsoring institutions should be
strong enough to ensure program continuity.

A summary of key insights and action steps concerning the financial
dynamics of incubators follows.

ACTION STEPS

FINANCIAL DYNAMICS OF INCUBATORS

1. The three models presented in this chapter are not mutually exclusive. A "best-practices" incubator will adopt the model, or combination of models, that best fits its own situation, i.e., that reflects expected outcomes, the number of high-growth potential companies in the community, the operating environment, and so forth.

2. Develop a realistic financial model that adequately reflects the operating characteristics of the incubator and the business environment in which it must operate. The model should account for all the operating and capital expenses, as well as the revenues.

3. Define a path to self-sustainability, which in turn should define the investments that must be made during the feasibility study, start-up and ramp-up phases.

4. Recognize opportunities for both current and deferred revenues, not only for financial reasons but also for their significance in recruiting and retaining a competent incubator president and staff.

5. Use the process of developing the financial model needs to be the catalyst for securing the commitments of sponsors to sustain the incubator until it can achieve financial self-sustainability.

4

Establishing Roles & Responsibilities of the Board

For those who make the decision to proceed with the development of an incubator, establishing the right board—structured correctly and focused on the mission of the incubator—is a critical success factor. The governance process can be an incredible distraction, or it can unify the commitment to focus on the development of companies.

BEST PRACTICE #4:

STRUCTURE THE INCUBATOR ORGANIZATION TO MINIMIZE GOVERNANCE AND MAXIMIZE ASSISTANCE TO INCUBATOR COMPANIES.

First and foremost, the board must accept its responsibility as the keeper of the flame. It must sustain the intensity of focus on the fundamental principles of successful business incubation—for its members, for the president and the rest of the incubator staff, for the community stakeholders and for the incubator companies. This chapter and this best practice are focused on the development of an operating board that will govern as efficiently as possible, in keeping with the principle of operating the incubator like a business. The board should add value beyond governance and maximize the commitment of resources to growing companies.

The discussion of the techniques for achieving these objectives can be framed by addressing the issues listed below.

Since sponsors of incubators typically respond to economic development needs in their communities and even sometimes to regional economic distress, a sense of urgency often drives them to get the incubator up and running as quickly as possible. For action-oriented individuals, the business of governance is often a distraction to be avoided. But for others, the incubator is a valuable public relations mechanism which can be used and abused. When sufficient care is not taken to establish the board correctly, the dis-

---

Key Issues of Governance

1. Roles and Responsibilities

2. Optimal Board Composition and Size

3. Operating Procedures

4. Structuring the Board

---

cord within the board and between the board and the incubator staff can be a significant barrier to success.

ROLES AND RESPONSIBILITIES OF THE BOARD

An incubator board has many roles and responsibilities, not the least of which is "keeper of the flame."

Develop and Update a Strategic Plan for the Incubator

The feasibility plan should provide the basis for the incubator's first business plan. However, once the incubator is functioning with a president and client companies, the board needs to develop a strategic plan to guide the long-term development of the incubator. The plan should be reviewed on a yearly basis and updated as necessary.

Set Policies Regarding the Board's Operation and the Role of the President

At a minimum, the board must fulfill its legal responsibilities with respect to governance in order to maintain its corporate and/or tax status. The board should include at least one director capable of ensuring these responsibilities are met. The board may be advised or required to retain outside legal counsel and/or an independent auditor. Similar concerns or responsibilities may be derived from requirements imposed as part of incubator financing. If these responsibilities are handled appropriately, the board may avoid the considerable distractions that can result from non-compliance.

There is probably no more important responsibilities for the governing board than developing the strategic plan and hiring the right president. (Chapter 5, which follows, is dedicated to helping sponsors fulfill this responsibility.) If the board hires a competent and effective incubator president, then the need for oversight by the governing board should be minimal. A periodic *pro forma* program review may be sufficient to satisfy reporting requirements of funding agencies and to provide incubator management and board members with the opportunity to make sure they are

Roles and Responsibilities of the Board

1. Develop and update a strategic plan for the incubator.

2. Set policies regarding the board's operation and the role of the president.

3. Manage external relations for the board and for the incubator.

   - Run political interference
   - Take the lead in marketing the incubator in the community
   - Work with the incubator president to establish and manage the know-how network of community experts
   - Buffer the president from the array of external distractions

4. Support the business operations of the incubator.

5. Support the development of the incubator companies.

keeping to plan and on budget. If maintaining the relationship between the board and the incubator president consumes more than minimal effort and if reasonable attempts to rectify the problem have failed, then it is the responsibility of the board to find a new president.

In addition to hiring the president, which is critical from both an operational and financial perspective, the board makes other decisions affecting the performance of the incubator program or may require that it approve certain decisions made by the incubator president. For example, the board should be involved in decisions related to acquiring the incubator facility, locking in the financial commitments of sponsors, and authorizing major capital expenditures. If the incubator president's compensation package includes participation in equity and royalty agreements with incubator companies, the board should reserve the right to approve those agreements as well.

In the beginning, the board will be involved in establishing policies that govern the relationship between the incubator and the client companies. Often these policies are reflected in the lease or program participation agreement that every incubator company signs upon entering the incubator. Generally, the board will also consider and approve revisions to these agreements based on operating experience, as well as exceptions to the standard agreements for certain prospective companies.

Whatever policies the board adopts should be minimally restrictive. A competent incubator president should be given as much latitude as possible in implementing the board's intentions. If the incubator president is less than fully competent, the board will have to impose more restrictive policies and spend more time on oversight. The result is a diversion of time and energy to compliance with policies, and less time and resources available for the companies—the antithesis of a best practices incubator.

Areas in which it is appropriate for the board to establish policies are outlined in Figure 8.

Manage External Relations: Run Political Interference

The board needs to take the lead in preserving positive and productive relationships between the incubator, the sponsors, and other external stakeholders. This may be particularly important when financial investment is required to sustain the incubator during the early stages of start-up and ramp-up, or where expectations may be unrealistically high.

Although the incubator may be most vulnerable when it is still competing for the financial support of its sponsors, there is always the danger that some individual or group may target the incubator program in order to capture part of its visibility, part of its cash flow, or even the job of the current incubator president. Having to deal with these kinds of issues can be a tremendous distraction for the incubator president. The board can and should intervene. Ideally, one or more directors will have sufficient clout to resolve these situations with minimal involvement on the part of the incubator president.

FAILURE IN BOARD LEADERSHIP

A newly hired executive director of a community board responsible for an incubator decided to siphon off cash generated by the incubator for other community projects. His action deprived the incubator of funds allocated for bringing the incubator building into compliance with safety and fire codes. The incubator president raised a stink with the board. The board was badly split over how to handle the crisis, and the executive director of the board fired the incubator president. Lawsuits were filed by the incubator president against the board and the executive director, and vice versa. The executive director eventually lost his job and the lawsuits were settled. However, the costs of litigation drained the incubator of cash, and the program was destroyed.

In this case, the board failed to fulfill its responsibility to run political interference on several counts. First, it did not develop and commit to a set of clear operating principles for itself and for the incubator. Second, it did not conduct adequate due diligence regarding the motivations and principles of the individual hired to be executive director. Third, it failed to muster the cohesiveness and decisiveness needed to resolve the crisis in its early stages.

Unfortunately, the single greatest source of political interference often comes from members of the board itself. Hence, selection of board members, recruiting of a competent incubator president and structuring of the relationship between them are critical to the incubator's success. Even

FIGURE 8

Policies Boards Need to Establish

1. Annual audits by legal and accounting professionals

2. Reporting requirements for the incubator president

3. Separation of duties between incubator staff and the board of directors

4. Terms of employment agreements with incubator staff

5. Compensation plans and schedules for staff

6. Limits on the power of the president to make financial and legal commitments without board approval

7. Admissions criteria and policies

8. Standard agreement(s) between the incubator and its companies, and the latitude the incubator president has, if any, in modifying these agreements

9. Approval of commitments and contracts that exceed the authority of the president

10. Reviews of the performance of the incubator and its staff

11. Consideration of succession planning, including provisions for apprenticing a successor during a transitional period

12. Risk management

when the incubator management and the board members do all the right things, personnel and priorities can change at sponsor organizations. Even long-term financial commitments can come under siege when the sponsoring organizations experience a change of leadership or a major change in their financial or political environment.

The best strategy for protecting an incubator against destructive political interference requires sponsors and the founding members of the board to:

- build the three principles and the best practices outlined in this book into the entire incubator program from the very beginning

- recruit stakeholders, especially board members and the incubator staff, who will commit to sustaining these principles and practices

The founding sponsors, board members and the incubator president must be vigilant to guard against loss of commitment to founding principles. The board members especially need to drive the incubator toward self-sustainability and then commit to staying in the game for the long haul—if the community is eventually going to enjoy the "harvest": growing companies that create jobs.

Manage External Relations: Take the Lead in Marketing the Incubator in the Community

Typically the members of an incubator board represent the leadership of a community from the business, academic and government sectors. The extended networks of these individuals are usually sufficient to identify more than enough prospective client companies for the incubator. Ideally, the board will appoint an individual or a committee specifically to generate these leads and to refer them to the incubator president.

While the board should set an admissions policy, it should let the incubator president implement admissions procedures. The president may request the involvement of board members and other advisers in making admissions decisions. But if too much time is spent on the admissions process, the business assistance program is deprived of the full attention of the incubator president. While the admissions process may be useful to prospective companies, the investment of the president's time in making admissions decisions should be minimized.

Manage External Relations: Establish and Manage the Know-How Network of Community Experts

Development and maintenance of the community know-how network can be a tremendous asset for an incubator but also a tremendous time drain for the incubator staff. On the positive side, the know-how network can be a source of critical information that a generalist incubator president often does not have at his/her fingertips. On the negative side, each network relationship requires investment of staff time and resources.

The incubator president must play an active role in establishing and managing the know-how network. However, there are some measures that can be taken to minimize the time investment of the president while maximizing the impact of this network on the incubator companies. For example, the network can be structured to reflect two levels of involvement. There may be a small core group of experts on whom the incubator president relies most of the time and for which the president takes primary responsibility for maintaining strong ties. The much larger extended group of know-how experts can and should be the responsibility of a board committee or selected members.

The board can provide a coordinating function to deal with the volume of inquiries from people interested in participating in the network, to provide a mechanism for screening resources and to manage the process of linking these resources to the incubator and the incubator companies. This role is especially appropriate for a retired business leader who is recruited to the board specifically to serve this function. This type of individual should have the time and community stature to be effective. In addition, the board can establish expectations for community participants, smooth things out when they don't go well, provide positive feedback and sustain involvement where that is appropriate.

Where the board does not have the capacity for this level of involvement, the business manager/coordinator will have to take more responsibility for managing the extended know-how network. One effective coordination technique is the development of a know-how network database or resource guide. Being listed in the guide can provide the recognition and "official stamp of approval" the know-how network experts seek, as well as an easy way for incubator company entrepreneurs to identify sources of assistance in the community.

Manage External Relations: Buffer the President from Multiple External Distractions

The distractions related to political interference, marketing and the know-how network are difficult enough for the incubator president. But members of the board can sometimes be additional sources of distractions. For example they often ask incubator presidents to:

- take an active role in other economic development activities, boards or committees that may have little to do with the development of incubator companies
- host visitors from all over the world who are interested in incubators,
- accept speaking engagements
- provide free consulting to companies outside the incubator
- be a clearinghouse for people seeking jobs
- connect members of the stakeholder network to consulting opportunities, not only with incubator companies but also with other members of the stakeholder network
- be guest lecturers or faculty in entrepreneurship classes at all levels of the educational system
- participate in regional, state and national associations and meetings on behalf of incubator sponsors

In each of these cases a competent and successful incubator president has much to contribute, and people can argue that there is some indirect benefit to the incubator program or its sponsors that will justify the investment of time. It is easy to say "yes" when asked to talk about the incubator and much more satisfying than trying to overcome the resistance of an entrepreneur who does not seek and sometimes does not want the assistance offered by the incubator president. However, if the time of the president is consumed with external activities and too little time is invested in assisting the incubator companies, the ultimate purpose of the incubator gets lost in the shuffle.

Board members should be aware of this time trap and be very cautious about asking the incubator president to take on "just one more assignment." Almost all of the activities listed above can be adequately discharged by board members and other stakeholders. Each commitment to external activities should be viewed as a tradeoff in time, recognizing that the president's primary responsibility is to spend time helping client companies.

POLITICS AND TIME MANAGEMENT

The government relations office of the primary institutional sponsor of an incubator arranged for the visit of a congressman to review various sponsor programs seeking federal support. Even though the incubator was not one of the programs seeking federal support, the congressman wanted to visit the incubator, and the sponsor asked the incubator president to roll out the red carpet. The potential for direct positive impact on incubator companies or the incubator itself was zero, but the sponsor institution had much to gain from the visit of the congressman. The incubator president spent the equivalent of several man-days to comply with the request of the sponsor representative on his board—days that he was not available to help client companies that needed his assistance.

REMEMBER: TIME IS THE SCARCEST RESOURCE

A regional economic development agency received state funding for a small business loan fund. The incubator president was asked to sit on the loan committee as a public service. The loan criteria were structured so that no incubator companies could possibly qualify. The time required to review the extensive loan applications and then to sit in on the review meetings consumed at least one day per month, with no direct benefit accruing to the incubator companies.

In each of these cases the participation of the incubator president could be justified in the name of maintaining sponsor relations, marketing the incubator within the community or establishing relations with potential funding agencies. Incubator governing boards often encourage their incubator presidents to participate in these types of activities; many incubator presidents believe they should participate in these kinds of activities. However, the result is a serious drain on the time the president has available for helping companies.

At issue is the tradeoff between the costs of participating (or not participating) in these activities and the benefits to the incubator and its client companies. Typically, the president devotes so much time to these external activities that he/she has too little time left to concentrate on helping companies in the incubator. The overt pressure on the incubator president to be externally oriented is reinforced by a more subtle underlying dynamic in the relationship between the incubator president and the entrepreneurs. Entrepreneurs often resist the "intrusion" of the incubator president. The incubator president often feels that he/she is "beating my head against the wall." By comparison, in the world outside of the incubator, the president is viewed as a professional expert and is appreciated for that expertise. It is easy to see why many incubator presidents respond to external pressures and avoid taking a proactive approach with incubator companies. They use external demands on their time to avoid jumping in where they may not be welcomed or trying to persuade entrepreneurs to accept advice that they do not want to hear.

There is no magic formula for striking the optimal balance between external activities and internally focused business assistance. The formula will vary from community to community and will also vary over time as the incubator passes through various stages in its own evolution. Even so, the governing board and the incubator president must be zealous in pursuing the optimal balance. It takes discipline, constant vigilance and a real commitment to ensuring sufficient attention to the needs of the incubator companies. The governing board needs to be part of the solution rather than the primary source of the problem.

Support Operations of the Incubator as a Business

Clearly, the incubator must sustain itself as a business if it is going to offer business assistance to incubator companies over the long haul. To minimize the dependence of the incubator on external financial investment and to conserve the president's time, some boards have found creative ways to support the operations of the incubator. For example, sponsors may be able to provide loaned staff and other resources to cover some of the costs related to business functions such as real estate management, accounting and facility maintenance.

THE VALUE OF A LOANED EXECUTIVE

A public utility, one of the three primary sponsors of an incubator, assigned a loaned executive to the incubator specifically to assist the incubator president in managing business functions, which included facilities management, accounting and acting as the custodian of the agreements between the incubator and the participating companies. Because he did not have to spend time on these functions, the president could spend more time working with the incubator's client companies.

Often the champion of an incubator who sits on the board has the latitude to provide non-cash support services, as long as the sponsor perceives value in participating in the incubator project.

Support Development of Incubator Companies

Board members, as well as other stakeholders, can serve as members of the incubator president's business assistance team, providing resources and expertise that complement and extend what is provided by the incubator staff. The purpose is to strengthen areas of weakness of individual companies and to compensate for their deficiencies. This kind of support can take a number of forms, including (1) participation on a company's board of advisors; (2) providing expert advice, such as legal or accounting; (3) acting as a liaison to resources in the network of the incubator and its sponsors, which may even extend far beyond the local community; (4) acting as an intermediary to potential customers, suppliers and joint venture partners; (5) helping identify prospective key employees; and (6) providing financial investments.

In many cases, the roles of the board members and other stakeholders may appear to be similar to the roles the incubator president plays in helping companies grow. However, the incubator president usually sustains more direct involvement and assistance on a more persistent and continuing basis than a board member or other stakeholder. Chapter 9 provides a detailed analysis of the process of identifying needs and providing assistance to incubator companies. The board member who is willing to engage in this type of involvement needs to work with the president to identify opportunities to provide assistance and to determine the best approach to use.

OPTIMAL BOARD COMPOSITION AND SIZE

All the board members, regardless of which stakeholder group they represent, must be committed to the three principles of business incubation and to avoiding conflicts of interest. These commitments must form the basis for a set of ethical standards guiding the behavior and performance of board members, individually and collectively. Board members must avoid the perception or reality of advancing their personal agendas and, instead, align their interests with those of the incubator.

The list of roles and responsibilities of the board presented earlier in this chapter suggests that some stakeholders may be more appropriate for inclusion on the board than others. That differentiation may be particularly important when the incubator has matured beyond the start-up phase, during which broad community involvement may be appropriate or necessary. An optimal board might comprise some or all of the "parties-at-interest" listed below.

Optimal Board Composition

- Leaders/Champions Committed to the Principles of Successful Business Incubation
- Networkers
- Real Estate and Business Operations Professionals
- Business Assistance Providers
- Investment Professionals
- Entrepreneurs
- Product/Service Assessment Professionals

Leaders/Champions Committed to the Principles of Successful Business Incubation

The commitment to the guiding principles of successful business incubation is important for all board members but especially so for the leaders of the board, who must have the discipline to inspire and sustain that commitment, i.e., champion the concept of the incubator. The board needs to include one or more champions with the capacity to lead and who command the respect and support of the remaining board members. In most cases, the board leaders will be members of the senior management team in the organizations sponsoring the incubator.

Networkers

Given the need to market the incubator and coordinate the extended know-how network, strong connections to an extended community network are desirable. Often these individuals are involved in organizations that provide services to the business community, and they often serve in sales, marketing or community relations capacities. These individuals also may be drawn from other community organizations that provide business assistance, such as a Chamber of Commerce, a S.C.O.R.E. chapter or a Small Business Development Center.

Real Estate and Business Operations Professionals

The two primary activities of the incubator staff are sustaining the incubator as a business itself and assisting incubator companies to become successful businesses. The skill sets required to be effective in these two activities are seldom found in the same individual. Given that the ideal incubator president will first and foremost be an expert at providing business assistance to start-up companies, it can be a great advantage to an incubator if one or more members of the board are knowledgeable about real estate and business operations. They can provide advice and oversight to the staff charged with these functions.

Business Assistance Providers

Some of the board members should have the capacity, the time and the willingness to be role models and facilitators for those stakeholders who will become directly involved in helping the incubator companies develop. These may include service providers, such as lawyers, accountants and business consultants, who can lend their expertise both to incubator companies and to the incubator itself. There will undoubtedly be a need to exercise caution regarding real or perceived conflict of interest, since the relationship of service providers to incubator companies can range from volunteer to fully paid professional adviser.

Investment Professionals

Given that financing new ventures is one of the most difficult challenges facing incubators and their companies, it is appropriate to include representatives of the risk capital and banking communities on the board, as well as wealthy individuals who have experience as angel investors.

Entrepreneurs

The individuals drawn from the categories listed above often have little experience in an entrepreneurial environment. The dynamics and practices employed in established businesses can be markedly different from those in entrepreneurial ventures. There is a significant danger in establishing a board that has very little experience with entrepreneurial business practice. Ideally some of the board members will have direct, or, at the very least, all will have indirect experience with the entrepreneurial process. Best-practices incubators appoint successful entrepreneurs to the board, ask other entrepreneurs for advice on particular issues and hire incubator presidents who provide entrepreneurial leadership.

Product/Service Assessment Professionals

For technology incubators (or incubators dealing with innovative products/services), it may be helpful to include individuals who are accustomed to evaluating technologies or products, e.g., intellectual property attorneys or directors of government/university/corporate research and development laboratories. These individuals can help the incubator president assess the products of prospective companies and are likely to know others who can be helpful in this regard.

The decision regarding the number of directors that should serve on the incubator board must be dependent on the community in which the incubator is located and the philosophy of the board. Begin with the smallest board possible to fulfill the requirements; then add additional members, after calculating the time that will be required by the incubator president and staff to support each additional member vs. the benefits that person can provide to the incubator and its companies.

OPERATING PROCEDURES

The frequency of board and committee meetings and the nature of the business conducted during the meetings are two issues related to operating procedures. Within the incubator industry, the frequency of regular board meetings ranges from monthly to annually. There are certain minimum requirements that must be met to retain corporate status, but beyond that, the value of board and committee meetings is to promote communication. When communication needs are more significant, e.g., during start-up, when major decisions must be made, during crises or when significant new members join the board, meetings may be more frequent. However, meetings and preparation for meetings consume a significant amount of time and energy of the incubator president, the incubator staff, the board members and outside stakeholders—and usually have little direct benefit to the incubator companies.

Best practice suggests that a board should be focused on (1) managing the business of the incubator and (2) working with incubator companies. This translates to the minimum number of board and committee meetings possible, commensurate with legal requirements and communication needs, meetings that are as short as possible and more time available for helping companies.

REMEMBER THE FIRST TWO PRINCIPLES

One incubator struggled in the early stages through a financial crisis, the defection of the first president, the shut down of the original incubator facility and the start-up of a new facility. The board, which had taken a laissez faire approach from start-up until the crisis hit, committed itself to a much more activist involvement with the new president. This translated into monthly meetings and resulted in a significant time commitment. The entrepreneurs perceived significant opportunities for beneficial relationships with the board members on a variety of dimensions, but the board members had no time left to work with any companies. A number of entrepreneurs were disgruntled that governance preempted the provision of the assistance they needed.

STRUCTURING THE BOARD

The Legal Form of the Organization

Approximately 90% of the incubators in the United States are not-for-profit. The cash flow derived from operating the incubator is directed at two primary incubator activities: sustaining the incubator as a business and assisting incubator companies to reach their full potential.

A variation on the separate not-for-profit corporation is the embedded organization, which is not a separate legal entity but operates within the context of a larger organization. It is not uncommon for an incubator to be part of a parent organization—frequently one of the founding sponsors — such as a university, a governmental entity, or a quasi-public economic development agency. Most often the parent is a not-for-profit organization.

In some cases embedded incubators work from a separate budget and are expected to account for both income and expenditures in order to meet budget. In other cases the embedded incubator is treated as a cost center, with an allocation from the parent. Often the parent organization will assume some administrative responsibilities and their related costs, such as those for accounting, legal assistance and insurance. Typically, embedded incubators have their own boards of directors or advisers.

The relationship between the embedded incubator and its parent organization (or between the stand-alone incubator and its dominant sponsor) can range from weak to strong and from positive to negative. The incubator and its companies may benefit from the infrastructure and resources of the parent organization or sponsor. However, on the negative side, the capacity of the incubator to act as an independent business and to be entrepreneurial can be compromised by the bureaucracy of the parent or sponsor.

Whether the sponsors decide to establish the incubator as a stand-alone, not-for-profit corporation or to embed it within a sponsor organization, there is no substitute for competent legal counsel. Make absolutely certain that the legal issues are managed correctly, and comply with IRS regulations required to retain the appropriate tax status. Also, whether the incubator is stand-alone or embedded, implementing the principles and practices outlined in this book can help the incubator achieve optimal performance.

The Operating Form of the Organization

There is no formula for creating an optimal organizational structure. Each incubator organization must find the structure and operating procedures that promote maximum adherence to the principles of successful business incubation. A number of variables affect the decision-making process regarding structure, including the orientation and capacities of the incubator president and members of the board, as well as the nature of the incubator's community environment.

While recognizing the importance of these variables, the following discussion is based on the premise that the incubator will have an activist board composed of individuals who are committed to fulfilling the roles and responsibilities identified earlier in this chapter. When those responsibilities are routine and recurring, the board may choose to establish standing committees composed of one or more board members and perhaps stakeholders. The committees might include some or all of the following:

Finance and Audit: This committee is responsible for ongoing financial review, including issues related to sponsor investment, capital expenditures, and equity/royalty agreements. This committee is a resource for the incubator president in the development of the annual budget and works with the president in resolving any audit issues.

Fundraising: Although this committee will generally be most active during start-up and ramp-up, when the incubator program still requires investment from sponsors, there may be a need for a fundraising capacity even after the incubator has achieved financial self-sustainability. For example, the incubator may undertake an expansion or major renovation that could require additional capital to be raised. Likewise, there may be reasons to pursue funding for special assistance programs.

Personnel: The Personnel Committee assumes responsibility for recruiting, selecting, and employing the incubator president. It also recommends personnel policies to the board (e.g., compensation, benefits, performance appraisal systems, and conflict-of-interest policies). This committee may take the role of advocate, adviser and supporter of the president and staff, and may conduct performance reviews of the president if the executive committee elects not to do so.

Legal Issues: This committee will take the lead in developing, monitoring and maintaining the various legal agreements associated with operation of the incubator, such as incorporation documents, lease and service agreements, employment agreements for the incubator president and staff and conflict of interest agreements.

Marketing and Community Relations: The Marketing and Community Relations Committee will recruit companies to the incubator and serve as a catalyst to make sure community resources are targeted to the incubator and its companies. This committee may also provide speakers and incubator representatives who can take the place of the incubator president at public functions and who can act as tour guides for visitors to the incubator.

Real Estate Management: At start-up this committee will take the lead in identifying appropriate facilities for the incubator and will lead the effort to plan and execute whatever activities are required to convert the facility to an incubator. Thereafter, it may participate in facility management or act as a resource to staff members charged with that responsibility.

Nominating Committee: The Nominating Committee proposes and recruits new Board members and manages the process of retirement of outgoing members and the election of others.

Business and Technical Evaluation Committee: Although routine participation of the Board in the client admission process is not recommended, incubator presidents may wish to have a board committee that can serve as an advisory resource for evaluating prospective companies. In the case of technology-based companies, the incubator president may also need people to help make technical evaluations of prospective companies, products or services.

Executive Committee: If the board is large, i.e., more than ten to fifteen members, it will be important to empower the executive committee to act for the board. It should also be charged with evaluating the performance of the president.

Other: For non-recurring activities, the board may form ad hoc committees as necessary.

An activist board composed of individuals committed to contributing significantly to the mission of the incubator—with minimal demands on the time of the incubator president—is desirable. However, an important trade-off reflecting common reality should be recognized: most volunteers, whether acting as individuals or as committees, require some level of staff support. The value added through the efforts of volunteers must be weighed against the value lost when the time of the president is diverted from companies to providing staff support to volunteers.

In its simplest form, the ideal relationship between the president and all the incubator's support structures could be represented by the diagram in Figure 9.

For most incubator presidents there is one additional relationship that is not depicted on this organizational chart, i.e., the relationship with the community. Managing this relationship can be very time consuming. However, the community is best served when the incubator president dedicates the maximum time possible to assisting companies, thereby increasing the probability of survival and success for as many incubator companies as possible. At the same time, the community often has a wealth of resources that can help both the incubator and the incubator companies. Leveraging stakeholders and the resources they can bring is the subject of the next chapter. An effective governance structure can be established by following the listed action steps.

FIGURE 9

An Organizational Structure for Effective Governance

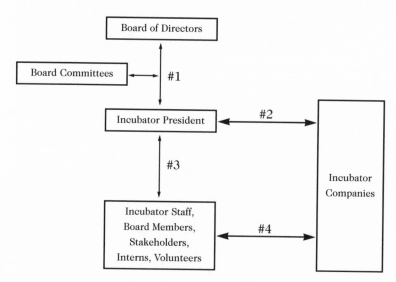

Recognizing the central and critical role played by the incubator president in most incubators, the incubator president, the board and the other
stakeholders should adhere to the following:

- Minimize the time required to sustain the relationship between
  the board and the incubator president (labeled #1 in the
  organization chart).
- Maximize the time of the incubator president dedicated to direct
  interaction with incubator companies (labeled #2).
- Minimize the time of the incubator president required to manage
  relationships with staff members, board members, interns and
  other stakeholders involved in the incubator (labeled #3 in the
  organization chart) with respect to incubator operations.
- Maximize the time of the staff members, board members, stakeholders, interns and volunteers devoted to helping companies,
  based on the roles and responsibilities they have agreed to play
  in the individual plan of assistance the president develops for
  each company (labeled #4).

ACTION STEPS

FOR ESTABLISHING AN EFFECTIVE GOVERNANCE STRUCTURE

1. Form a not-for-profit organization, either as a stand-alone corporation or embedded in a not-for-profit parent. Secure competent legal counsel to make sure the approach is implemented correctly.

2. Select board members who will commit to the principles underlying best practices: focus on the development of companies and operate the incubator like a business.

3. Hire a competent incubator president who will require minimal oversight.

4. Make decisions about the size of the board, frequency of meetings, length of meetings so as to minimize the investment of time and resources in governance, oversight and communication and to maximize the investment in growing companies.

5. Create an organizational structure that pushes the activities of the board down to the committees and individual board members.

5

Managing the Stakeholder Network

When an incubator is in the feasibility study and start-up phases, involving a broad spectrum of community stakeholders is often necessary for survival. In fact, broad-based community support often motivates sponsors to invest financial resources. However, as the incubator moves up its own growth curve, its relationship with community stakeholders needs to evolve and change. The reason for involving stakeholders changes from garnering support for sponsor investment to focusing community resources on helping companies grow.

BEST PRACTICE #5:

ENGAGE STAKEHOLDERS TO HELP COMPANIES AND TO SUPPORT INCUBATOR OPERATIONS.

Early in the process of developing an incubator, the incubator staff and board need to establish a healthy relationship with the community, based on an appropriate set of expectations regarding the nature of the relationship. In a healthy relationship the flow of time, energy, resources and support is primarily one way, i.e., from the community into the incubator. This helps the incubator support the growth of companies, which will have a positive economic impact, including the creation of jobs in the community. By contrast, in an unhealthy relationship, community stakeholders view the incubator as a vehicle for advancing their own agendas and the incubator staff as their public servants. Unfortunately this kind of relationship is fostered when the staff of a poorly planned and implemented incubator depend on stakeholders to keep their financially marginal incubator on continuing life support.

The concepts listed below are useful to structure the discussion of stakeholder management.

Managing the Stakeholder Relationship

1. Understand the tradeoffs between the costs and benefits of engaging the stakeholder network.

2. Optimize the inter-relationships among stakeholders, the incubator president and the incubator companies.

3. Establish roles for stakeholders.

4. Implement strategies for effective management of the stakeholder network.

THE COSTS AND BENEFITS OF THE STAKEHOLDER NETWORK

For most incubators, engaging the stakeholder network as broadly as possible during the feasibility and start-up stages is an important strategy for testing the market and the willingness of potential sponsors to commit sufficient investments. However, if the incubator is structured to achieve financial self-sustainability by the end of the ramp-up stage, then the relationship between the incubator and the stakeholder network should change as the incubator matures.

Most incubator presidents subscribe to the great networking myth, i.e., they believe they have to maintain an extensive community network in order to operate a successful incubator. There is a widespread belief in the incubator industry that the more extensive the network, the more value the president can deliver to incubator companies. Incubator presidents often boast about how many bankers, professors, lawyers, consultants, government officials, accountants, student interns and so forth are part of their stakeholder network.

Without doubt the stakeholder network offers access to resources and "know-how" that entrepreneurs often do not have but definitely need. However, having access to hundreds of network contacts is a far cry from having the ability to tap those individuals who can have a significant impact on the growth of a particular company.

One of the challenges for the leadership of an incubator is to maximize the benefits while minimizing the cost of networking—which is primarily the time of the incubator president to develop, sustain, and manage the stakeholder network. The benefits are access to and acquisition of resources and expertise that can improve the probability of survival and success of the incubator companies. But the costs can be significant.

OPTIMIZING THE RELATIONSHIPS

Many stakeholders and communities unwittingly take more from the incubator than they contribute to it. Often stakeholders consume large amounts of the president's time and fail to effectively deliver resources and expertise that help develop the incubator companies.

There are many reasons for this:

- Some stakeholders get involved in an incubator to push their own personal agendas rather than a community-wide agenda related to helping companies grow.
- Some stakeholders seek visibility in the political arena or look for a public relations channel to "market" their own products or services.
- Some incubator presidents and board members do a poor job of facilitating connections—often because they do not have enough time and persistence.
- Some network contacts do not have the expertise or the resources they profess to have or are unable or unwilling to "deliver" resources when needed.
- Some entrepreneurs do not have the interest or the capacity to take advantage of stakeholder involvement.

The two extreme networking constructs are illustrated in Figure 10, "Allocation of Time for Business Incubation." Each circle represents the "best" way and "worst" way for the president, companies and stakeholders to allocate the time available for business incubation.

While quality and quantity of time spent directly assisting the incubator companies are both important, without sufficient time there will not be the intensity and persistence needed to move companies through "the incubation process."

ESTABLISH ROLES FOR STAKEHOLDERS

As suggested in the preceding chapter, sponsors, board members and other community leaders can play key roles in developing, sustaining, and managing the network. The effectiveness of board members and key sponsors can be extended by the effective involvement of other stakeholders. Consequently, many of the roles identified for board members in the prior chapter may be appropriate for stakeholders who are not board members.

For example, marketing the incubator to the community is an obvious role that stakeholders can fulfill, either as leaders of the effort or in support of a board committee established for that purpose. Stakeholders can watch for potential incubator candidates and encourage entrepreneurs or companies to apply for admission to the incubator. Start-up entrepreneurs often approach professional service providers, lawyers, accountants, and bankers who should be encouraged to refer these entrepreneurs to the incubator.

In addition, since facilities management and operations are time consuming, stakeholders may be able to free up some of the president's or staff's time by volunteering to assist with these functions. If these activities are

![FIGURE 10]

Allocation of Time
for Business Incubation

BEST CASE: Maximize A,B, & C — Minimize X & Y

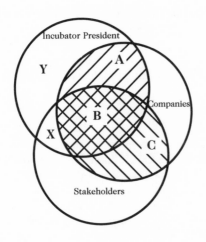

Best Case

A + B: Over half of the incubator president's time is dedicated to working with companies and/or with stakeholders to implement the plan of assistance for companies.

B + C: Over half of the stakeholders' time is dedicated to working with companies, implementing their roles/responsibilities in the plan of assistance for each company.

X: A small portion of the stakeholders' and president's time is spent interacting with each other on activities unrelated to helping companies.

Y: Less than half of the president's time is spent on operational activities that are unrelated to helping companies.

WORST CASE: Maximize X & Y — Minimize A

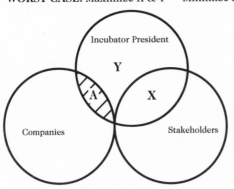

Worst Case

A: Only a small percentage of the incubator president's time is dedicated to helping companies.

X: The time required for networking between the stakeholders and the incubator president with no direct benefit to the incubator companies is substantial.

Y: More than half of the president's time is spent on activities that are unrelated to helping companies.

coordinated through a board committee or board member, volunteers can be recruited to work with them.

EFFECTIVE USE OF STAKEHOLDERS

When an incubator was ready for the move up to a new and bigger building, the incubator president found herself without the expertise to manage the build-out required to transform the building into an incubator center. A local engineering firm volunteered its services to ensure that the contractors got the job done right, saving the incubator money and the incubator president valuable time she could then spend working with client companies.

Finally, there are many ways stakeholders can help support the development of incubator companies, including:

- providing expert advice to incubator clients as part of the community know-how network
- providing advice on an ongoing basis, perhaps as a member of an advisory board or as a mentor for an entrepreneur
- serving on a legally constituted board of directors
- investing in one or more incubator companies
- conducting training programs
- providing preferential pricing treatment to incubator companies as either a buyer or supplier of goods and services
- developing opportunities for co-marketing to common customers

Stakeholders are typically the workhorses of the "know-how" network. They can be a tremendous resource for the incubator as it tries to help incubator companies compensate for their deficiencies. Given the limited amount of staff, hence time of the incubator management team, the stakeholder network can provide incubator companies with accounting, financial, management, legal and intellectual property advice and counsel on sales and marketing, human resources and production management. If members of the know-how network can be convinced to provide their services *pro bono* or at a discount, so much the better for the incubator companies.

IMPLEMENT STRATEGIES FOR EFFECTIVE MANAGEMENT OF THE STAKEHOLDER NETWORK

These strategies can be summarized as (1) encourage board members to coordinate the involvement of stakeholders; (2) recognize and be responsive to the needs of stakeholders; and (3) use a two-tiered approach in managing the stakeholder network.

Encourage Board Members to Coordinate the Involvement of Stakeholders

Whenever stakeholders assume direct and continuing roles in supporting the development of the companies, they need to work through the structure developed by the incubator president and/or the board. Usually this means working through a board committee or a designated board member with responsibility for coordinating the stakeholder network. Coordination is especially important when there are multiple relationships between a given company and those who are trying to help it: the incubator president, board members, members of the know-how network and other business assistance organizations.

In the best of all worlds, the stakeholders add maximum value to the companies with minimum involvement of the incubator president.

HOW TO PROVIDE MORE SERVICES

One incubator has developed a close working relationship with a regional economic development organization that receives public and private funding to manage a network of volunteer business advisers. Although this organization typically focuses on established manufacturers and technology-based firms, it has taken the initiative to work with some of the incubator's companies. In turn, the president has encouraged incubator companies to plug into the network of business advisers by working directly with the regional economic development organization where and when appropriate. The president of the incubator maintains an active communication channel with the staff of the other regional organization and many of its volunteers. Neither group suffers from a "protect your turf" mentality. The two organizations actively look for opportunities to collaborate, e.g., in sponsoring training programs that can serve their overlapping constituencies.

Recognize and Be Responsive to the Needs of Stakeholders

Although community service can be a simple and powerful reason for stakeholders to support a community incubator, it is important to recognize other motivators, including:

- the potential impact on a stakeholder's business related to the positive public relations gained from involvement in the incubator and its successful companies
- the opportunity to establish relationships with incubator companies that may eventually grow up to become substantial clients or customers

The incubator president and the board committee or member responsible for managing the stakeholder network need to be cognizant and respectful of these motivations. When a stakeholder has added value to the incubation process, the stakeholder should be rewarded by having its needs met, whether that means gaining public recognition or the facilitation of connections with other incubator companies. The challenge for the incubator president is to meet the needs of the stakeholder efficiently, recognizing the tradeoff between time spent meeting the needs of stakeholders vs. time spent working with client companies.

Use a Two-Tier Approach in Managing the Stakeholder Network

The incubator president should identify and maintain close ties to a small core group of service providers—the first tier of the stakeholder network—who can meet 90% of the needs of incubator companies, who are willing to respond quickly and who require minimal facilitation on the part of the incubator president.

When the needs of the companies go beyond the capabilities of the core group, the incubator president should be able to turn to a contact on the board responsible for coordinating the stakeholder network. That board committee should make every effort to sustain the extended community network at a lower level of intensity and activate the connections only as the need arises. Since the second tier of extended contacts will likely be involved much less frequently than the first tier of core experts, the board members or incubator president may need to be more involved when there are interactions between a company and the second tier of the stakeholder network.

The following are steps for effective management of the stakeholders network.

ACTION STEPS

FOR EFFECTIVE MANAGEMENT OF THE
STAKEHOLDER NETWORK

1. Keep the focus on the companies. Do not network for the sake of networking. Start with a small core group that is prepared to act like a SWAT team to intervene quickly and decisively under the direction of the incubator president.

2. Secure commitment from the board members, the stakeholders and the incubator president to limit the amount of time the president allocates to networking that does not directly benefit an incubator company.

3. Develop a committee of the board that will take the lead responsibility for all other networking functions, including:

   - building and sustaining the extended community network of second tier know-how experts and accessing that network when help is needed that the core group cannot provide
   - representing the incubator on other community boards, hosting guests, conducting incubator tours, providing media exposure, etc.

4. Challenge members of the stakeholder network to help where they can have the greatest impact on the success of the incubator, i.e., with marketing the incubator, supporting operations, and directly helping the companies.

6

Building the Incubator Management Team

The central mission of a business incubator is to help entrepreneurs start and grow their companies. The incubator—both as a facility and as a program—provides a mechanism by which the incubator president and staff, the board members and the other stakeholders can accomplish that mission. But the incubator itself must do more than survive in order to accomplish its mission. If it is going to serve as a strong, stable launch pad for start-up companies, it must be a successful business in its own right. If the president focuses time primarily on working with incubator companies, the other staff must be able to manage the business functions of the incubator, with the assistance of board members and other community stakeholders, as appropriate.

BEST PRACTICE #6:

RECRUIT STAFF WHO WILL MANAGE THE INCUBATOR LIKE A BUSINESS AND A PRESIDENT WHO HAS THE CAPACITY TO HELP COMPANIES GROW.

Incubators which have difficulty in achieving financial self-sustainability tend to focus on operations, i.e., maintaining the organization rather than assisting client companies or customers. A best practices incubator is structured and staffed to function like a self-sustainable business and is focused on serving its customers, i.e., helping its client companies grow. These two goals may be accomplished by addressing the following staffing issues.

DESIRABLE CHARACTERISTICS OF AN INCUBATOR PRESIDENT

An incubator is a start-up, an entrepreneurial venture in its own right, with the incubator president cast in the role of entrepreneur. Howard Stevenson at the Harvard Graduate School of Business defines entrepre-

---

Key Staffing Issues

1. Desirable characteristics of an incubator president

2. Structuring the compensation package to recruit and retain an ideal incubator president

3. Effective strategies for staffing an incubator

4. Optimizing the incubator workload

---

neurship as "the pursuit of opportunity without regard to the resources currently under one's control." The "pursuit of opportunity" is high risk, with a high degree of uncertainty and a rapid pace of change—all common characteristics of business incubators.

Most sponsors are established governmental, economic development and/or educational institutions, for whom the practices and the culture of entrepreneurship are unfamiliar—even unknown. They are more comfortable with the principles and practices of program management and real estate management. Problems occur when they hire someone with the skills of program and real estate management—because the skills needed to manage an existing program or facility are much different from those required to help entrepreneurs. Figure 11 describes the characteristics of a "Best Practice" incubator president.

The difficulty of hiring a president with the right mix of entrepreneurial capacities and experiences is illustrated by the case of a university incubator.

PRESIDENTS ARE ENTREPRENEURIAL LEADERS

Following the resignation of the first full-time incubator president, a search committee was formed, an executive recruiting firm was retained and a nationwide search was initiated. After the initial scan of the hundreds of resumes, the search committee decided to interview the top six candidates. Following two rounds of interviews, the field was narrowed to two finalists.

One candidate had followed a traditional career path up the ladder of a large management consulting firm. He had excellent communication skills, a strong network within the university community and a track record of accomplishment in business. But his track record included no evidence of entrepreneurial experience, orientation or capacity. The other finalist also had excellent communication skills and a strong network within the university community. But his track record had "no track." He had been a co-founder and president of an entrepreneurial

FIGURE 11

Characteristics of a
Best Practices Incubator President

1. All the personality characteristics of an entrepreneur, including high energy, high need for achievement, persistence, capacity to learn from mistakes, drive to keep moving ahead, adaptability, strong work ethic, self-confidence, self-starting capacity, and the ability to operate independently with minimal direction.

2. A personality that includes the qualities of caring and high integrity.

3. Some experience as an entrepreneur or with entrepreneurship, and the skills and wisdom that come with that experience. Some experience with failure.

4. High tolerance for the low probabilities of success coupled with a "mad dog" drive for success reflected in a total commitment to the process of helping entrepreneurs grow their companies.

5. Excellent communication, sales, negotiating, decision-making and networking skills.

6. Superior mentoring, teaching and advising skills.

7. Dynamic motivational and leadership skills.

8. The business savvy necessary to help companies grow, including competence in finance, team building, sales/marketing, the product development process and the strategies of business development.

9. The business savvy to help the incubator make it through its own start-up and become financially self-sustainable.

10. The capacity to develop a strong community and extended network.

start-up, had done some small business consulting, had taught in public school and had been an investment counselor in a large financial institution.

The search committee was very comfortable with the "career track" candidate but less so with the entrepreneurial candidate. The entrepreneurial candidate had to work hard to convince the committee that his eclectic experience was an asset rather than a liability. Ultimately he was hired and went on to achieve significant success in revitalizing the incubator program.

In spite of the difficulties the sponsors and board may have in finding and selecting the right president, it is one of the most critical tasks they will undertake. The board of directors needs to hire an individual who is so committed to the process of helping entrepreneurs grow their companies that he/she views all other tasks as an intrusion on the central mission. The president must ensure that the basic business functions are executed in order to build a firm foundation from which to provide business assistance to the companies and accomplish this objective with the minimum expenditure of resources. This person must thrive on the risk and uncertainty associated with start-up and must understand the dual challenges of developing a successful incubator and successful incubator companies. He/she must be sensitive to the needs of individual companies at different stages of their development and be able to help them find the resources required for growth.

Finally, the president should have the toughness and wisdom to understand and accept the realities of the business creation and development process: most companies will succeed but some will fail—despite considerable investments of time and energy by the incubator president, staff and network. It is also important to recognize that success and failure are relative terms. Success can encompass fast growing "superstar" companies; strong, profitable small businesses; and "lifestyle" (or "Mom and Pop") businesses that provide employment but might be considered marginally profitable. Businesses that do little more than survive can be considered a success from a business incubation perspective if survival gives the entrepreneur time to learn and grow in entrepreneurial skills that may lead the venture beyond survival, or which may be applied to developing a successor venture. Even helping an entrepreneur fail inexpensively can be considered a success if it avoids a spectacular and costly disaster and if it provides the entrepreneur with knowledge and wisdom that comes out of learning from mistakes, disappointments and failures. An incubator president may have relatively few venture capital-type home runs, but in a best practices incubator most entrepreneurs will find themselves part of the success spectrum described above.

Venture capitalists, with experience in picking winners, review 1,000 business plans to find 10 in which they are willing to invest. Only one or two out of the ten are home runs. By contrast, a best practices incubator might enable a "winner" to grow faster than it would on its own. But even a best practices incubator will not produce 100% winners. Finding and selecting a president who can be effective in this demanding, high-risk environment is not an easy task.

It may seem that the ideal incubator president must walk on water, and sponsors and board members may conclude that it will be impossible to find someone who meets the criteria outlined in the previous section. Of course, no single individual is likely to have all these qualities and capabilities, but successful incubator programs are generally led by people with enough of those qualities and capabilities to be effective. The Appendix includes profiles of five of those individuals, the contributing authors of this book.

STRUCTURING THE COMPENSATION PACKAGE TO RECRUIT AND RETAIN AN IDEAL INCUBATOR PRESIDENT

A best-practices incubator will pay fair market compensation to attract and retain the talent required to successfully implement best practices. Compensation surveys conducted by Coopers & Lybrand indicate that too often incubator boards try to pay incubator presidents salaries that are appropriate for program administrators or real estate managers, typically $25,000 to $50,000. As the old adage suggests, they usually "get what they pay for." In those cases where the board succeeds in attracting a president who fits the optimal profile detailed in the first section of this chapter but provides inadequate compensation, the incubator president soon moves on to a position for which the compensation is more commensurate with his/her talents. In fact, turnover of talented incubator presidents appears to be a significant current challenge for the incubation industry.

Depending on the employment market and the extent of responsibilities assigned to the president, the board should expect to provide a base salary somewhere between $50,000 and $100,000, with a benefits package appropriate for a business development professional in this salary range. In addition, the president should have the opportunity to participate in a significant way in any royalty/equity pool derived from agreements between the incubator and its companies.

Experimentation with royalty/equity agreements is still in the early stage, and there are not yet any "best practices." In addition, there are potential conflict-of-interest issues which must be acknowledged and addressed. The board should work with compensation advisers, legal professionals and industry experts to develop a plan which they will need to modify as experience with this type of compensation plan accumulates. However, participation in such a plan can stimulate and motivate an incubator president and staff to work hard to help incubator companies be successful, knowing that they will have an opportunity to participate in the upside potential of these.

Alternatively, some boards may feel reluctant to distract themselves from the other complex and considerable challenges of launching a best-practices incubator. The board may choose to appoint a committee to work with the president in developing a proposal or set of alternative proposals to address royalty/equity positions in the president's compensation package. The board and staff need to take the time to look at existing models of royalty/equity participation and understand the ramifications of these issues before deciding whether and how to incorporate royalty/equity "kickers" into the compensation package.

EFFECTIVE STRATEGIES FOR STAFFING AN INCUBATOR

The Incubator President

Hiring the incubator president early in the process enables that individual to participate in decisions critical to the success of the incubator:

- selection of a facility
- hiring of additional incubator staff
- structuring governance procedures
- early stage marketing of the incubator to the entrepreneurial community

The timing of the president's hiring must be related to the financial model that is adopted and the sponsors' level of financial commitment. Hiring the president earlier in the development process may increase the start-up costs. Having the president on board early may also shorten the ramp-up period, thereby providing cost savings. A competent, dynamic leader will increase the emotional and financial commitment of sponsors to the project; speed up the process of acquiring the facility, systems, equipment and staff; and increase the sense of momentum of the incubator project in the community. All this can increase the rate of applications and acceptances of client companies who decide to locate in the incubator.

If the financial model requires a certain level of cash flow before hiring a president, then the sponsors must find someone, e.g., a loaned executive, who can assume the role of incubator president on an interim basis, either part-time or full-time.

The tasks of a best practices incubator president include:

- counseling (for certain companies at particular stages of development)
- preparing entrepreneurs to take advantage of external resources
- linking the companies to external resources
- providing the intensity and persistence necessary to get the companies to make the best use of counseling and access to these resources

The Operations or Business Manager

Establishing effective management and operations systems early during the start-up and ramp-up phases pays significant dividends down the road. This is as true for the incubator as it is for the companies in the incubator.

All participants in the incubator—client companies, advisers in the know-how network, board members and staff—should expect the incubator to be a model business operation.

An operations or business manager need not be full-time in the beginning and might be a loaned executive, a competent volunteer working on a *pro bono* basis, or a paid staff member—if the budget will allow. If the business manager is a full-time paid staff member, his/her annual base salary should be in the range of $30,000 to 50,000.

The operations or business manager must excel at administering the range of activities listed in Figure 12, "Allocation of Incubator Staff Workload." The individual must be task-oriented and have the discipline to execute tasks from start to finish. The business manager must be a self-starter, requiring minimal oversight by the incubator president. Above all else, this individual must have exceptional people skills, since she or he will have more day-to-day contact with more incubator company employees about more issues than anyone else. It is essential that this person be competent to perform these tasks; otherwise the incubator president will have to compensate for any shortcomings in performance—which will diminish the capacity of the president to provide assistance to companies, i.e., to achieve the First Principle.

The Secretary/Receptionist

The secretary/receptionist is also critical to the success of the incubator. Usually this person is the first contact that people on the outside have with the incubator or the incubator companies. Many incubators provide receptionist and telephone answering services to the client companies. When the number of participating companies grows to ten or more, the management of phone calls to the incubator and the companies, coupled with the volume of visitors to the incubator, will pre-empt secretarial duties. When this happens, other arrangements will need to be made to accommodate the secretarial demands of the president and incubator companies.

Until this time, the secretary/receptionist may be able to help companies with word processing, can service the business equipment, order supplies, manage the mail and faxes, etc. Since this individual has significant daily contact with entrepreneurs and their employees, he/she is likely to be the first to know when things are going right or wrong. In most markets the board should expect to pay $15,000 to $25,000 for a competent secretary/receptionist.

The following characteristics are desirable in the incubator secretary/receptionist:

- high energy and a strong work ethic
- caring personality with a high level of integrity
- professional demeanor and appearance
- excellent communication skills, both for phone and in-person contacts

FIGURE 12

Allocation of Incubator Staff Workload

S = Secretary/Receptionist   OM = Operations or   P = President
                                    Business Manager

TASKS	PRIMARY RESPONSIBILITY		
	S	OM	P
Secretarial Duties:			
• Clerical Functions	Δ		
• Telephone Answering	Δ		
• Receptionist Duties	Δ		
Operations Manager:			
• Facility Management		Δ	
• Leasing		Δ	
• Maintaining Shared Services/Facilities		Δ	
• Managing Student Interns		Δ	
• Marketing to Prospective Tenants/Visitors		Δ	
• Accounting and Finance		Δ	
• Purchasing		Δ	
President:			
Key Relations Management:			
• Board/Sponsors			Δ
• Know-How Network			Δ
Assisting Incubator Companies:			
• Counseling/Mentoring			Δ
• Networking to External Resources			Δ
• Creating the Environment for			Δ
Entrepreneurial Success			

- high tolerance for working in a "fish bowl," with phone calls and people coming in, non-stop, from all directions
- word processing skills
- other secretarial skills

Expanding Beyond a Core Staff

Significant financial support from sponsors is difficult to sustain long term; therefore, most incubators must rely primarily on cash flow from their own operations. Since this limits the staff that can be hired to provide direct assistance to companies, there is considerable motivation to reach out to external sources of business assistance. Best practices incubators do not expand beyond the core staff described above unless they receive funds from sponsors to do so or are provided with executives on loan.

Student interns represent an excellent opportunity for incubators and their companies to gain access to talent at a minimal financial cost, but there are some tradeoffs, as noted in Figure 13.

EFFECTIVE USE OF GRADUATE STUDENT INTERNS

One incubator established a relationship with the school of business at a local university and has linked teams of students with incubator companies for the past five years. In more than 90% of the projects, the participating companies reported that the value gained has significantly exceeded the cost. Students most commonly perform marketing studies, but other assignments include the preparation of financing plans, business plans, and cost accounting systems. One student team prepared financing documents that a company used to acquire bank financing. A team of Taiwanese students used their contacts in Taiwan and Japan to prepare a plan for a small manufacturing company that had tried to penetrate the far east marketplace but failed to gain entry to that market.

Where student intern programs have been successful, the participating faculty and students view the incubator companies as their customers. The programs are focused on two ends: giving the students an opportunity to gain experiential education by working with an entrepreneurial company; and delivering a useful product to the incubator companies. Further, successful internship programs include sufficient supervision by the faculty and involve representatives of the participating companies, hence minimize the time required of the incubator president.

OPTIMIZING THE INCUBATOR WORKLOAD

The tasks of operating an incubator fall into two basic categories: those activities related to running the incubator like a business and those focused on helping incubator companies grow. In a best practices incubator, the

FIGURE 13

Tradeoffs in Student Intern Programs

Potential Benefits

1. Access to talents and skills that may be in short supply within the entrepreneurial team.

2. Opportunity to try out potential future employees.

3. Supervision by someone else, e.g., faculty or staff at the college or university.

4. Valuable assistance at favorable rates. (In fact, if students are receiving credit, the cost to the participating companies may be close to zero.)

5. Development of a pool of entrepreneurial talent that may be a source of new ventures as well as employees for entrepreneurial companies.

Potential Downside Risks

1. Costs in time of the entrepreneur and other key employees to orient students to the company's mission, market and products.

2. Costs in time of the incubator president to work with the students and the representatives of the college or university who manage the program.

3. Misdirection of a company if the results of a student project are of poor quality yet are implemented.

---

incubator president is focused primarily on assisting companies as much as possible. Therefore the rest of the incubator staff and volunteers, e.g., board members, stakeholders and interns, should handle the business functions related to operating the incubator, under the general direction and oversight of the incubator president.

The incubator staff's functions can be divided into those that can be handled by a secretary/receptionist, those that may be appropriate for an operations or business manager and those that should command the attention of the incubator president.

In incubators where board members and other stakeholders volunteer support, the operations manager may be able to take on significant responsibility for managing key relationships, thereby allowing the president to allocate additional time to assisting companies. However, even in the best of circumstances, i.e., with a very capable operations manager and an active, self-managing group of volunteers, the incubator president will have to spend 20% to 30% of his/her time on operations and key relationships management.

Unfortunately, the current practice is for the demands of governance and incubator management to consume most of the president's time. The typical president currently spends 20% or less of his/her time directly assisting companies. This is simply not enough time devoted to the central mission of the incubator: helping entrepreneurs develop their companies. Given a good board, competent staff and a well-managed stakeholder network, the president of a best practices incubator should be able to spend at least 50% of his/her time directly assisting companies.

CHOOSE A PRESIDENT WHO CAN HELP COMPANIES GROW

The president of a midwestern incubator was focused on helping his incubator company entrepreneurs. Entrepreneurs credited him with providing assistance at critical stages in their development. However, they also complained that the basic real estate issues, e.g., security and maintenance, were poorly managed. When the president left, the incubator board reacted to the complaints about facilities management by selecting a new president more oriented toward real estate management. The tenants soon realized that they had a better managed facility but were receiving very little business assistance from the new president. Several of the most promising ventures moved, some closed down their operations and most of the rest are barely in survival mode.

Clearly board decisions regarding staffing must address both fundamental principles. The incubator must have the capacity, through the leadership of the president, to assist companies, and it must also have the capacity to effectively manage its business functions. The action steps required to build an effective incubator management team are outlined in the following.

ACTION STEPS

FOR BUILDING AN INCUBATOR MANAGEMENT TEAM

1. Start by developing an understanding of the business operations and business assistance tasks that must be accomplished to achieve best practices.

2. Establish a board committee whose responsibilities include staffing the incubator. Include individuals who have experience with business assistance programs and/or entrepreneurial environments. If necessary, utilize consultants to add expertise to the committee.

3. Develop a compensation package for the president and other staff members that will allow the incubator to recruit and retain the best.

4. Decide how much of the incubator workload can be accomplished by volunteer board members, stakeholders and interns; then develop a plan and secure commitments from them to implement the plan.

5. Within the limitations imposed by the financial model, hire the incubator president as soon as possible after the "to be or not to be" question has been decided affirmatively and after the group charged with recruiting the president is prepared to accomplish its task.

6. Make certain the incubator president and board committees responsible for staffing work together to complete the staff recruiting effort.

7

Selecting the Optimal Incubator Facility

It is not necessary to have a building to have business incubation. There are a variety of business assistance programs provided by many different organizations, from those that are publicly supported, such as Small Business Development Centers, to those privately supported, such as Chambers of Commerce. Even the National Business Incubation Association explicitly recognizes "incubators without walls."

However, entrepreneurs report that a primary benefit of being in a business incubator is co-location, which provides the opportunity to talk and work with other start-up entrepreneurs, to learn from each other, to share the ups and downs, to share resources and to trade with one another. These things happen more easily if the companies are in close proximity, i.e., in an incubator facility. The building also enables the incubator to achieve its revenue goals through sub-leasing portions of the building to tenant companies.

BEST PRACTICE #7:

CHOOSE A BUILDING THAT WILL ENABLE THE INCUBATOR TO GENERATE SUFFICIENT REVENUE AND ALSO SUPPORT BUSINESS INCUBATION.

A wrong decision regarding the choice of incubator facility can outweigh right decisions about the financial model, the governance structure and the incubator president. Even though the incubator building gets the most attention during the feasibility and start-up stages, all too often a sub-optimal building is chosen.

There are a number of reasons that the "facility" question gets so much attention from sponsors:

- Community leaders interested in economic development believe they understand real estate and the dynamics of real estate rentals better than they understand "business incubation" or growing companies.

- Bricks and mortar represent a tangible manifestation of the hard work and financial investment that goes into getting an incubator started. The sponsors can invite people to the grand opening, cut a ribbon and have something concrete to display.

- Business incubation activity can seem like black magic. The process of growing companies is uncertain, and growth is much less "tangible" than a building.

- Entrepreneurship is a lot more art than science; it is often messy. Most community leaders have difficulty understanding the process.

Unfortunately, too many people think that getting the building up and running is the end of the process of developing a business incubator—rather than the means to an end, i.e., one component in the whole system of support for growth companies. The right building can provide the basis for the financial self-sustainability of the incubator and an environment in which the entrepreneurs and incubator staff can work together to grow new businesses. The wrong building can lead to failure—and wrong buildings are one reason incubators have not met expectations.

The challenges of choosing the right facility can be summarized in the ten questions outlined in Figure 14, "Questions to Ask When Qualifying an Incubator Facility."

The first six questions let sponsors ascertain whether the facility will allow the incubator to become financially self-sustainable. The real estate related costs, from acquisition to operations, need to be sufficiently low compared to real estate related revenues to enable the incubator to achieve a balanced budget. The last four questions will allow the sponsor to determine whether the facility will meet the needs of the incubator's customers, i.e., incubator companies.

When considering a building, review historical records such as a statement of zoning classification, as-built drawings with revisions, inspection reports, utility and tax bills, the record of capital improvements and the plan by the current owner for anticipated capital improvements. In addition, talk with the building manager and/or maintenance supervisor to confirm operations and maintenance costs and discuss other operational concerns. If the sponsors do not have staff qualified to make judgments about the suitability of a building to house the incubator, then enlist volunteer or paid professionals with the necessary expertise.

SIZE

There must be enough area available for rental to companies, at or near market rates, to generate the cash flow required in the business plan. Therefore, either the building must be large enough from the start, or the area set

FIGURE 14

Questions to Ask When
Qualifying an Incubator Facility

1. Does it meet the size requirements of the financial model to enable the incubator to achieve self-sustainability?

2. Does it require minimal renovation?

3. Are there any environmental hazards that will come back to haunt the incubator later?

4. Can the facility be easily maintained?

5. How much will it cost to operate the facility?

6. Are the acquisition terms favorable or will the long-term costs cripple the incubator?

7. Can walls be moved and spaces reconfigured as companies grow?

8. Are there enough common areas that can be shared, e.g., conference rooms, a library, a kitchen and a business service center?

9. Is the incubator building and its surrounding area safe and secure so that entrepreneurs can work day or night?

10. Is there adequate parking?

---

aside for an incubator must be expandable. Size requirements can be determined using simple math. For example, assume the business plan requires $200,000 in revenue derived from leasing space to companies. Other assumptions include an average occupancy rate of 90%, an average collection rate of 95% and an average rental rate of $8 per square foot. The result is obvious: a building with 30,000 square feet of net leasable space is required. (See Chapter 3 for more detail on the development of financial models.)

RENOVATION

All too often an unsuitable building is made available at no or low acquisition costs. However, the costs of renovation or modification can be more expensive than the cost of acquiring a more suitable building. Make sure the costs of renovation fit into the financial model.

Entrepreneurs want space and surroundings that are adequate, but they need not be plush.

Dr. Pier Abetti, one of the founders of the Incubator Program at Rensselaer Polytechnic Institute, suggests that: "The rate of innovation is inversely proportional to the thickness of the carpet!" An adequate but not too comfortable facility can help motivate client companies to move through the start-up stage quickly in order to graduate to more upscale quarters.

Some of the best incubators have moveable walls and linoleum on the floor. Hence, sponsors need not do more renovation than is necessary. The space must meet the needs of the tenants who are starting up their companies, must meet building codes and must be safe. However, if too much money is invested in renovation, it places an unnecessary burden on the short-term and long-term finances of the incubator.

ENVIRONMENTAL HAZARDS

Environmental hazards can kill an incubator. The costs of removing environmental hazards are typically beyond the capacity of an incubator budget. The building selected must have a clean bill of health, or acquisition/occupancy must be conditional on the elimination of environmental hazards—before the incubator locates in the building.

THE WRONG FACILITIES CAN RUIN AN INCUBATOR

One incubator located in an old factory facility in a run-down industrial district discovered two buried, leaking gasoline tanks. The incubator budget was forced to bear the $50,000 cost of removing and disposing of the tanks. This issue exacerbated the discord between the president and the board. The incubator president was fired, and most of the incubator companies left the incubator.

MAINTENANCE

The building needs to be maintainable, both within the context of the budgetary model and within the time and capacity of the staff and volunteers. The incubator tenants will not expect the facilities to be maintained like Fortune 100 corporate headquarters, but they will expect that needed repairs will be made promptly and that the building will be kept clean. This is another area where the costs of maintaining an old building with old heating, ventilating, air conditioning (HVAC) systems; dealing with safety and security problems; repairing malfunctioning elevators and so forth can offset favorable acquisition costs. The costs of routine maintenance and eventual replacement of office equipment and building systems also need to be incorporated into the budget model.

OPERATING COSTS

Too often incubators are saddled with old buildings that are black holes with respect to energy consumption. The real costs of operating the HVAC systems, in addition to the costs of maintaining these systems, should be taken into account in the budget model. If energy usage varies substantially from tenant to tenant or is excessive for the types of tenants the incubator expects to attract, then make provisions for the costs of installing individual meters in the spaces to be subleased to these companies.

HVAC COSTS CAN BE A TIME BOMB

The old classroom building converted into an incubator center did not have central air conditioning. Carefully selected window air conditioning units enabled the utility bills for the building to be maintained at about 50 cents per square foot annually. But when the incubator expanded to the first floor of another building, which had been used as a corporate laboratory and clean room, the air handling requirements were so severe and the old HVAC systems so antiquated that the annual energy costs increased to approximately $2.50/square foot, well beyond the tolerance of the financial model. In the short term, an incubator sponsor is underwriting the utility costs of the new building, but both the president and sponsor know that this situation cannot be sustained. The president is currently seeking $400,000 in state economic development funding to remove all the existing HVAC equipment and to replace it with modern, energy-efficient equipment. If the state does not fund the renovation, the sponsor will abandon the facility, and the incubator will have to shrink and lose its access to laboratory space that complements the office space available in the original incubator building.

In addition to utilities costs, other operational costs, such as those for telecommunications systems, computer systems and taxes, need to be identified and accounted for in the budget model.

ACQUISITION TERMS

It is essential to know who makes the decision with respect to the transfer of ownership or the issuance of a lease. A long, drawn-out set of negotiations about the building will sap the energy and enthusiasm of the incubator development team. The terms need to be favorable and meet the numbers specified in the model that will enable the incubator to achieve self-sustainability. This is another area where real estate and legal expertise will be critical.

SPACE CONFIGURATION

A best-practices incubator with optimal tenant mix will become home to a variety of incubator companies requiring different-size spaces, from small spaces for start-ups with no capital to thousands of square feet for anchor tenants. In addition, a certain percentage of companies will be growing quickly, and others may need to shrink quickly when "the big order" gets delayed or does not materialize. Look for buildings where existing rated fire walls define zones within which some relatively inexpensive subpartitioning is possible.

The building should have the capacity to accommodate the progression of company growth, with "cubbyholes" of a couple of hundred square feet or less, step-up spaces of 300 s.f. to 500 s.f., spaces of about 1,000 s.f. and then some larger spaces of 2,000 s.f. to 3000 s.f. While anchor tenant spaces can be much larger, the incubator will be vulnerable if it leases too much space to a single tenant, thereby running the risk of a serious cash flow crunch if that tenant departs.

Figure 15 provides an example of the space allocation in an incubator with 35,000 square feet of leasable space. These are actual numbers from the incubator used as a case study for the real estate financial model in Chapter 3.

Chapter 8, "Recruiting and Selecting Client Companies," provides more information about the types of companies that will typically be recruited to an incubator to fulfill its two primary objectives: (1) providing a basis for incubator financial self-sustainability and (2) stimulating the development of job-creating companies. For example, out of the first three types of companies listed in Figure 15, six of the 24 companies might have high growth potential and sufficient maturity to warrant aggressive, proactive intervention by the incubator president. The president might spend four hours a week with each of these firms (24 hours total) in order to boost them onto the path of fast growth toward success. All the other companies (in this example, the other 27 companies) would receive a total of six hours per week. Strategies for providing proactive assistance are discussed in Chapter 9, "Making the Difference: Serving Client Needs." Flexible space configuration is essential in order to respond to the changing needs of companies as they grow.

COMMON AREAS

Although common areas are non-revenue producing space, the facility must have these areas to effectively promote interaction among tenants. If these are not available, entrepreneurs often complain that the building has no library, lunch room or common meeting area. Unfortunately many incubators get the worst of both situations—too many wasteful, non-rentable common areas in the form of hallways and stairways and too little of the

FIGURE 15

Configuration of 35,000 sq. ft. Incubator

Type of Company	# of Spaces	Size of Spaces	Total s.f.
Small Start-Up Service or Software Firms	5	300 s.f.	1,500
Micro-Manufacturing Start-Up Firms (and Established Small Software Firms)	15	500 s.f.	7,500
Early (Stage) Growth Firms	4	1000 s.f.	4,000
Growth Firms Nearing Graduation and Small Anchor Firms	5	2000 s.f.	10,000
Anchor Tenants	4	3000 s.f.	12,000
Total Leasable Space			**35,000**

space that encourages entrepreneurs to congregate and communicate.

SAFETY AND SECURITY

Some buildings and some neighborhoods can create security nightmares for the incubator management. The costs of providing adequate security must fit within the budget model, and if not, the prospective facility must be rejected.

SECURITY IS ESSENTIAL

An incubator company left an important package in the mailroom for pickup. Because of poor security, someone from the neighborhood wandered into the incubator, took the package and threw it into the incubator's dumpster. Fortunately the entrepreneur spotted the package when leaving the incubator at the end of the workday and retrieved it. Otherwise, the loss of the shipment would have created a significant disruption in the relationship with an important customer, if not the loss of that customer altogether. The lack of adequate security in this incubator made it difficult to retain current tenants and to attract new tenants.

PARKING

Incubator companies and the incubator both need to operate like real businesses. Real businesses provide parking for their employees, for their visitors (customers, service providers, investors, etc.) and for delivery vehicles. One rule of thumb suggests that there should be one parking space for each 300 s.f. of leasable space. The analysis of parking requirements should be based on the kinds of companies that will be recruited and their particular needs. For incubators housing companies manufacturing products, availability of loading docks and freight elevators are similarly important. When an incubator is embedded within a parent organization, organizationally and locationally, it will be important to negotiate an agreement related to parking. This is especially the case for university incubators, where parking is often a difficult challenge and where regulations that may be appropriate for students are not appropriate for the needs of businesses.

Acquiring an appropriate building will be facilitated by using the suggested action steps.

ACTION STEPS

FOR ACQUIRING AN APPROPRIATE BUILDING

1. Start by developing a workable financial model that will dictate the size of the building as a function of real estate revenue requirements.

2. Identify candidate facilities on the basis of favorable acquisition costs that can support the financial model—with an adequate margin of safety.

3. Undertake a complete and professional facility review to determine the condition of the building and its systems as a basis for analyzing renovation and operating costs. Pay particular attention to problems related to the presence of potential environmental or safety hazards.

4. Ensure that the facility can be adapted to meet the needs of the anticipated mix of tenants and the operational dynamics of a business assistance program.

8

Recruiting & Selecting Client Companies

There are three components in the delivery of business assistance:

- the incubator as a business entity, with a business plan, a financial strategy and governance structure
- the incubator team, including sponsors, community stakeholders, a board of directors and an incubator president and staff
- the facility which houses the incubator and the companies

All three are focused on the customers—the client companies that will locate in the incubator and/or receive incubation services. Hence, a major question for all incubators is: What strategy should be used to acquire the optimal mix of client companies?

BEST PRACTICE #8

RECRUIT AND SELECT CLIENT COMPANIES THAT PROVIDE REVENUE REQUIRED BY THE FINANCIAL MODEL AND HAVE THE POTENTIAL TO GROW AND CREATE JOBS.

To implement this best practice, consider the following guidelines.

MARKET THE INCUBATOR AND ITS PROGRAMS

In some rare cases, where the visibility is high and the community network extensive, an incubator may not need to aggressively market its programs and services.

BUSINESSES MUST MARKET—INCLUDING INCUBATORS

One five-year-old incubator with twenty-five client companies has been very successful at building and sustaining visibility in the entrepreneur-

---

The Process for Recruiting & Selecting Incubator Companies

1. Market the Incubator and its Programs

2. Structure the Admissions Process

3. Develop Admissions Selection Criteria

4. Achieve Optimal Outcomes from the Admissions Process

---

ial community and with the stakeholder network. Each year, hundreds of prospective incubator companies submit business plans. Rather than marketing, the greatest challenge has been managing the business plan review process. However, even this incubator has developed marketing materials, and it continuously and proactively markets its programs.

Most incubators will not have a steady stream of applications flowing through the door. In some cases, it may be more like a trickle. Many will feel pressure to admit companies to fill up the space so as to generate rental income to meet cash-flow requirements. The incubator president will need to take an active role in marketing the incubator during the start-up and ramp-up phases. However, after the incubator is established, an incubator marketing team can be created that includes board members, sponsor champions, members of the know-how network, the incubator staff and the incubator president. If the participants of the team are willing and able to take on an active marketing role, then the president can minimize his/her time commitment to marketing and focus on assisting incubator companies. If not, the incubator president will have to commit more time to marketing. In either case, the president must invest enough time to ensure a sufficient flow of client companies to sustain the financial health of the incubator.

The incubator president can help promote the marketing in the following ways:

- create marketing methods and materials that are user-friendly for team members, especially with respect to the first steps of the referral process
- reinforce desired performance early in the process and often by contacting the team members and asking for their referrals
- submit articles to the local paper or get stories on radio/TV about the incubator and its client companies in order to maintain the visibility of the incubator
- establish simple, clear qualifying criteria so that people will know which companies to refer to the incubator as prospects

- invite entrepreneurs from client companies to provide testimonials concerning the value of the incubator

For those involved in marketing the incubator, the following questions should shape the marketing effort:

1. What does the incubator have to offer prospective clients?
2. Where should the incubator be promoted?
3. What marketing channels are most effective?

What Does the Incubator Have to Offer Prospective Clients?

When the incubator is just starting, "credibility" in the eyes of prospective tenants can come only from (1) the record of the success of other, similar incubators; (2) the "halo effect" from the reputation and commitment of the incubator's champion(s) that transfers trust and credibility to the incubator; and (3) the special services and advantages the incubator offers which meet the needs of entrepreneurs. Later in the incubator's life cycle, a proven track record will serve as its most powerful selling point.

According to the National Business Incubation Association, as of 1994, there were approximately 500 incubators throughout the United States. Making prospective tenants aware of relevant facts about the incubator "industry" can help sell them on the merits of the incubator concept, even if a new incubator does not yet have a track record of its own. By being associated with this growth industry, any start-up incubator will benefit from the recognition that incubators are a powerful means of supporting small businesses and increasing their chances for success.

Attracting tenants is often an important outcome of the feasibility study process. By the end of a successful feasibility study, the stakeholders will understand the concept of an incubator and will begin identifying and recommending entrepreneurs or prospective client companies who may be likely candidates for the incubator and its programs. In any case, an incubator can further leverage the time and efforts invested during the formation stage by encouraging supporters to promote the incubator to potential tenants. In doing so, the incubator stakeholders provide the incubator with a "stamp of approval" by publicly supporting this new endeavor.

Identifying the needs of small and start-up businesses that are not being fulfilled by the current economic development infrastructure is another important outcome of the feasibility study. A well-designed "menu" of services that addresses these unmet needs will attract quality tenants. Some best practices incubators actually recruit companies and organizations that can provide these services to locate as "anchor tenants" in an incubator. Proximity to tenants such as a seed capital fund, a local Small Business Development Center, a university technology transfer office, a regional SBA office and a branch office of a law and/or accounting firm can be a plus when recruiting companies. These organizations can also be helpful to the president as he/she tries to identify and deliver the services that companies need for their growth.

Once an incubator has traversed the start-up phase, its ability to attract tenants will be a function of its demonstrated success, as well as its ability to reformulate its services as client companies' needs change. After its first two or three years, the incubator must be able to demonstrate more than the support of its champions. The incubator will be judged on its own record of success or failure. Prospective companies will be convinced of the benefits of locating in the incubator only if other tenants have received value and recommend the incubator and its services.

Where Should the Incubator Be Promoted?

The incubator can achieve name recognition and attract the attention of potential tenants through speeches, seminars and promotional material aimed at a variety of target audiences. Listed in Figure 16 are a few of the appropriate audiences to target.

What Marketing Channels are Most Effective?

The three primary marketing channels utilized by successful incubators are (1) speeches and seminars, (2) the media, and (3) written material for distribution.

Seminars and Speeches

In any community there are a multitude of business and service clubs, trade associations and educational institutions that are always looking for professional speakers with a good story to tell. The members of the incubator's marketing committee should respond to opportunities or contact the program chairpersons of these organizations and offer to speak.

Incubators that sponsor seminars and workshops that address the needs of potential client companies have found them to be effective recruiting tactics. Topics that typically draw large crowds include "How to Write a Business Plan" and "Financing Your Business." More specialized seminars can focus on any number of topics, including "How to Give Effective Presentations," "How to Maintain Intellectual Property Protection" and "How to Expand into International Markets." The target audiences for these seminars might be the Women's Business Association, MBA and other graduate students, managers of large corporations being restructured, current entrepreneurs and those who provide services to entrepreneurs. In the beginning, the incubator may need to tap into the mailing lists of stakeholder organizations, but it should develop its own mailing list over time. Appropriate mailings, stories in the local media and telemarketing should all be used to attract companies to the seminars. Routine follow up and cultivation of those entrepreneurs who attend can stimulate a flow of applications to the incubator.

Some incubators charge a nominal fee to attend their seminars; others

FIGURE 16

Target Audiences

1. Economic development organizations and programs:
   - local chamber of commerce
   - local and regional government economic development offices and programs
   - small business development centers
   - chapters of the Service Corps of Retired Executives (S.C.O.R.E.)
   - corporate economic development offices (e.g., utility and communications companies)

2. Business firms that traditionally work with start-up companies as clients or service companies that fit the incubator's special profile:
   - banks
   - venture capital groups
   - investment capital networks
   - Accounting firms
   - lawyers
   - outplacement firms

3. Organizations and individuals that promote general community awareness of economic development:
   - business writers for the local media
   - civic and service clubs
   - university student organizations, and
   - churches and other community organizations

4. Current incubator clients:
   - the best (and sometimes the worst) referrals can come from an incubator's current clients. Satisfied and enthusiastic clients are an essential component of the incubator's effort.

offer them for free in order to attract the greatest possible number of attendees and get exposure to potential customers. Co-sponsoring these seminars with other local service providers allows the incubator to reduce the cost and burden of organizing them and strengthens the incubator's ties with these professionals, many of whom may well provide referrals in the future.

The Media

The press is a cost-effective and time-efficient way to reach a large audience. Journalists represent an important segment of an incubator's network. Keeping them supplied with up-to-date news about the tenants, the incubator, its services, its upcoming programs and the achievements of its client companies does them a service as well. Apart from the local television channels, newspapers and business journals, the publications of the local and state economic development organizations, venture capital clubs and universities can all be appropriate vehicles for publicizing the activities and opportunities of the incubator.

Written Materials

Because the incubator needs to be managed as a business, professional-looking marketing materials are essential. These could include a brochure, monthly newsletters, flyers promoting seminars and eventually a videotape. Maintaining an up-to-date mailing list of interested individuals and organizations will keep the incubator's materials targeted to an appropriate group of prospective tenants and supportive professionals. These materials should be distributed whenever speeches and seminars are given and whenever the incubator receives visitors. In many cases, sponsors have contributed "in-kind" services by helping develop and produce these materials.

STRUCTURE THE ADMISSIONS PROCESS

The admissions process should provide an efficient and relatively smooth passage of client companies into the incubator and prepare them to take advantage of the incubator's programs and services. Many incubator presidents spend a disproportionate amount of their time on the admissions process—which detracts from the time they should be spending on the development of client companies and adds only minimal value to the companies applying for admission.

Best practices incubators structure the admissions process in stages. The first stage is characterized by information exchange. First, the prospective client company needs to gather enough information to make the decision about whether to apply for admission to the incubator. Then, a board member or the incubator operations manager, not the president, provides a tour of the facility and information about the incubator and the admissions process. If the company appears to be a likely prospect, the entrepreneur should be encouraged to make a formal application.

During the second stage, the entrepreneur prepares and then submits a preliminary business plan and/or application. In many cases, the entrepreneur receives feedback on the plan, makes revisions and resubmits the plan. At this stage, the review of the business plan may be conducted by members of the board and/or volunteer mentors/reviewers from the business community, MBA student interns and/or the incubator operations manager.

At some point, depending on the effectiveness of the other reviewers, the incubator president must get involved. In addition to reviewing the plan and application him/herself, the president may ask others to review the plan to assess the technology, market niches, business strategy, and so forth. At this stage, there are several issues to be addressed:

Strengths and weaknesses of the plan and the company: Are the strengths sufficient to enable the company to have a good chance at success? Do the weaknesses warrant outright rejection of the applicant? Is there a clear understanding of how the incubator can help the company address the weaknesses?

What segment of the incubator company population does the prospective company represent?: Since different segments of the population require different packages of targeted assistance, it is important to categorize prospective companies and estimate the amounts and types of assistance they will need. This issue is addressed in considerable detail later in the chapter.

Expectations: What are the expectations of the incubator president regarding the performance of the company and vice versa? This discussion of expectations is essential. The expectations the president has for a Small Business Development Center, a technology transfer company, a small software company and a small manufacturing company will be markedly different. The entrepreneur and the incubator president need to be honest about what each expects from the other.

Lease and program participation: Can the incubator president and the entrepreneur agree on the terms of the lease and/or program participation agreement? Is the entrepreneur willing to pay the current costs of locating in the incubator and the current and deferred costs of the incubation services, i.e., is he/she willing to share equity, royalties or some portion of the income stream?

The admissions team needs to guard against the danger of making the application process too cumbersome. Even with a very effective and efficient application process, there is still a substantial requirement for gut-level judgment about a company's potential for success and job growth. The president should focus more on the entrepreneur's (1) commitment, (2) follow-through on agreed tasks, and (3) recognition of the need to gain access to services and professional assistance—and less on the proposed product or service. A committed, capable entrepreneur can adapt to the market and will utilize assistance to improve the product and make the venture succeed.

DEVELOP ADMISSIONS CRITERIA

The admissions criteria should reflect the principles underlying best practices in business incubation. Companies admitted to the incubator should help the incubator achieve the revenue required in its financial model, hence enable the incubator to operate like a business. With the exception of "anchor tenants," they should also have a high potential for growth and job creation and therefore warrant the intense and focused assistance that the incubator can provide.

The pool of potential incubator clients should be screened, using criteria such as:

- capacity to pay for the space and services they receive
- relative potential for fast growth
- type of business
- willingness to accept and act on advice and counsel

Capacity to Pay for Space and Services
If the incubator is going to succeed as a business, client companies must pay their rents and fees on a regular basis in accordance with the financial plan the incubator has developed to achieve self-sustainability. While there may be a few exceptions or a few extenuating circumstances, the general rule should be that companies which cannot pay their rents and fees on time or within 30 days must leave the incubator.

Some companies will be able to pay for space and services and will require both. Others, such as anchor tenants, will be able to pay for space and services but will use few services. Small start-up companies may need small amounts of space and few services in the beginning. The incubator must assess each company's needs and ability to pay and structure the rental arrangements in ways that will serve the incubator and the company.

Relative Potential for Fast Growth
The only way to justify the creation and expense of an incubator is to accelerate the development of companies so they grow, create jobs and contribute to the development of the economy. Since helping high-growth companies achieve their potential is the most efficient and effective way to achieve job growth, best practices incubators will search for and admit those companies with the best prospects for growth. While not all companies in the incubator need be fast-growth (e.g., anchor tenants will likely be stable) a significant proportion should be growth-oriented companies. The tradeoff is obvious: each tenant that demonstrates slow or limited growth potential occupies space that could be used to foster rapid-growth companies.

Attracting fast-growth companies is also important in order to create the right expectations and culture within the incubator. If the incubator simply provides assistance to marginal companies or admits mostly "lifestyle" companies, it will not be able to attract and retain the kinds of companies which will enable it to achieve its mission. The following story is a case in point.

SELECT AND ADMIT COMPANIES THAT WANT TO GROW

When one entrepreneur left the incubator, he commented that he had joined the incubator expecting to find like-minded entrepreneurs committed to growing highly successful ventures. He had hoped that other entrepreneurs would stimulate and challenge him and provide him with an opportunity to learn from their collective experience. Instead he found an incubator populated primarily by engineers and scientists who were only interested in playing with their technologies and building better "mouse traps." They hoped money would magically appear on their doorsteps so they could continue to lead the lifestyle of an inventor rather than build a business. The entrepreneur was disappointed with his incubator experience and was not shy about expressing his disappointment in the community, thereby making it more difficult for the incubator to attract other potential high-growth companies.

Type of Business

Type of business is an important dimension for segmenting the population of prospective companies. The most successful regional economies are built around clusters of companies in similar or related technologies or markets (sometimes call the "agglomeration" phenomenon). Research suggests that the more entrepreneurs "run in packs," the more successful they can be because they can share supply sources and distribution channels, buy and sell to each other, co-venture on contracts and attract employees with similar technical skills. This helps explain the development of regional economies such as Silicon Valley and Route 128. Hence, the more an incubator can attract similar or related companies, the better the chances each one has of being successful.

However, this sometimes means that an applicant may actually be a competitor of a current tenant in the incubator. Some incubators develop procedures to ensure friendly coexistence of competitors and promote collaboration. Other incubators simply do not admit a company that is a direct competitor of a current incubator tenant. However, significant potential synergy can be created by admitting companies that might be competitors—if the conflicts can be managed. An incubator program may develop some degree of expertise in facilitating the marketing or distribution of certain products or services. For example, co-location of businesses that provide services or products to the health care industry can enable all of them to learn from each other and acquire information that will benefit their individual marketing efforts. Once an incubator staff has helped one light manufacturing business successfully negotiate shelf space for its product in Wal-Mart or Kmart, other companies seeking those distribution channels could benefit from the expertise gained by that experience.

HOW COMPETITIVE TENANTS CAN COLLABORATE

One incubator has chosen to develop a cluster of woodworking companies. At first glance, these companies appear to be competitors; however, they have worked out a set of mutually beneficial relationships. One of the companies is the anchor tenant for the incubator facility, and the owner serves as a mentor to the entrepreneurs of the woodworking start-ups. He subcontracts some of his work to them and gives them access to some of his equipment. This enables him to solve production-capacity problems, and the start-up companies have been able to jump-start their businesses with the cash flow from their subcontracting work.

Willingness to Accept and Act on Assistance

An entrepreneur's willingness to accept and act on the advice and counsel of the incubator president is closely tied to the potential impact of the incubator on the survival and relative success of the company. Start-up companies that have the capacity to pay their rent but have no interest in capitalizing on the assistance programs of the incubator should not be admitted.

ACHIEVE OPTIMAL OUTCOMES FROM THE ADMISSIONS PROCESS

The results of a best practice incubator's admissions process are described in the box.

Sufficient Flow of Companies

Generally, the incubator must admit enough companies to generate the revenues required, based on the financial model that has been adopted. Too much selectivity can restrict the flow of incoming companies and sooner or later create cash flow problems for the incubator. The need to generate cash flow for the incubator and the desire to admit only high-growth potential companies creates a dynamic tension that incubator boards and presidents must continually balance.

MANAGE THE INCUBATOR AS A BUSINESS

One incubator president was told the incubator should be highly selective and that he should try to "pick winners" among applicants to the incubator. However, in performance reviews it became clear that he would be measured on the financial viability of the incubator. When some members of the incubator advisory board questioned the wisdom of admitting anchor tenants or companies that had little prospect of immediate growth, others reminded them of the importance of balancing the cash-flow needs of the incubator with the desire to admit all fast-growth companies.

Realistic Expectations

Incubator companies need to know what they will get in exchange for their current rent payments, service fees and equity or royalty commit-

Results of Successful Admissions Process

- Sufficient flow of appropriate kinds of companies into the incubator program

- Realistic expectations regarding what the incubator can deliver to each company and what is expected of each company

- Minimization of the numbers of hours invested per company reviewed and admitted

- Segmentation of the client companies in an effort to maximize the impact of the incubator on each company

ments to the incubator. They also need to know and to accept the incubator's own performance expectations. These expectations will vary, depending on the company, but might include the following:

- prompt payment of invoices for rent and services provided by the incubator
- compliance with the terms of the lease and program participation agreements
- attendance at meetings hosted by the incubator for training, sharing information or other purposes
- a willingness to talk with visitors who are touring the incubator
- provision of financial and other reports to the incubator president and participation in monthly or quarterly review sessions
- a commitment to doing their best to implement their business plan

The development of a business plan and clarification of expectations between the incubator president and client company are important aspects of the admissions process.

Segmentation of the Incubator Population

Since the resources of most incubators are limited, the incubator president needs to target different types of assistance to companies, depending on their needs. The goal is to maximize the impact of the incubator on the companies and thereby help them grow and create jobs. One way to do that is to categorize prospective companies according to their level of maturity and growth potential.

Since the admissions process includes a careful review of each company's business plan, the incubator president should assess each company's critical success factors with regard to: (1) the management team, (2) the product or service and related operations/manufacturing, (3) the market, and (4) financial capacity or understanding of the requirements to grow the company. Assessing the maturity of the company with respect to these critical success factors will enable the incubator president to segment the client companies according to the framework presented in Figure 17.

Using this framework, the incubator president can categorize incubator companies in order to determine how much staff time and assistance will be required. The president should then analyze each company within these four categories with respect to its critical success factors; determine what needs to be strengthened, corrected or eliminated and develop a plan of assistance for each company.

Group I: Superstars

The Superstar companies will be the most attractive. Their products or services will be nearly developed and ready for an established market in which there are already many potential customers.

These companies will require relatively little assistance from the incubator president. However, they may need introductions to financing sources, phone calls to open the door to a strategic alliance, help with recruiting and developing the management team and possibly flexible space that can be reconfigured, as needed, to fit the company's growth pattern.

A SUPERSTAR COMPANY

One incubator company began in an entrepreneurship class that required teams of students to develop written business plans. Thanks to

FIGURE 17

A Framework for Defining an Optimal Mix of Incubator Firms

Level of Maturity of the
Firm With Respect to
Critical Success Factors

		High	Low
Growth Potential of the Firm	High	I. Superstars	II. Up-and-Comers
	Low	IV. Anchor Tenants	III. Long Shots

intensive assistance from key champions in the incubator and other sponsors, the company survived on a shoestring for the first couple of years and then entered a period of fast growth. For the past five years, its sales have more than doubled every year, and it has been profitable in every quarter. The company now employs over 200 people and has recently gone public.

WHY SUPERSTARS NEED INCUBATORS

One founder of a fast-growth company commented that he wished he could have started his company in an incubator, thereby relieving himself of any concerns about space, phones, furniture and business services so he could concentrate on developing the product and hiring people.

Although Superstar companies typically do not require much proactive assistance from the incubator president, there are opportunities for the incubator to have a positive impact. These kinds of companies significantly enhance the reputation of the incubator as a place that adds value to companies, and they provide role models for less mature incubator companies.

Group II: Up-and-Comers

The Up-and-Comers can benefit most from proactive assistance provided by the president and other stakeholders. These firms have sufficient current or potential competitive advantages to qualify them as potential Group I: Superstars. If the incubator has resources to help overcome their weaknesses or deficiencies and if the incubator president commits to intensive involvement with these companies, some of them can be moved from Up-and-Comer status into the Superstar category.

FROM UP-AND-COMER TO SUPERSTAR

One incubator company started up when three managers were fired by their company. They knew the market and the strengths and weaknesses of their former employer's product. At start-up, the company was an Up-and-Comer with significant hurdles to clear that included building a competitive product from scratch, acquiring technical talent to complement the business talent of the founders and securing sufficient investment to survive until the product was ready to market. The incubator helped on all three counts, and today the company's revenues exceed $50 million annually.

Having an incubator full of Up-and-Comers is not realistic. They would require more energy, assistance and time than a president and staff could provide. But an incubator with no Up-and-Comers is an incubator without much hope of future-growth companies.

Group III: Long Shots

Long Shot firms are accepted by the incubator for several reasons. A candidate company might have latent capacities that the entrepreneur is still trying to convert into competitive advantages. If the company is able to pay rent, the incubator president may choose to admit the company and assign it to the Long Shot category. Long Shot firms typically need a supportive environment and time for the entrepreneurs to make their way through the earliest stages of the entrepreneurial learning process. Often the Long Shot entrepreneur is largely unresponsive to direct intervention, learns best through his/her own experience and from other entrepreneurs, and therefore does not require much proactive assistance from the incubator president. Just being in an incubator and around other entrepreneurs adds considerable value.

FROM LONG SHOT TO UP-AND-COMER

One Long Shot entrepreneur was accepted into his incubator because of his proven capacity to develop a service for a large and growing market. In an interview conducted several years after start-up, he admitted that he needed a couple of years of stumbling around on his own before recognizing the difference between developing a service and building a company. At that point, he became aware of the value of tapping the assistance of the incubator and took the initiative to access it. He began to make the transition to the Up-and-Comer group of incubator companies.

Sometimes the cumulative impact of various factors that comprise the incubator environment causes Long Shot firms to break out of the pack and move to Up-and-Comer status. However, many of these firms never mature beyond the Long Shot stage and will either be marginal survivors, lifestyle companies, or will run out of resources and give up. Given limited incubator resources, Long Shot firms should receive little or no proactive intervention assistance from the incubator staff unless and until they show promise and potential for moving into the Up-and-Comer group. Their status in the incubator should be reviewed on a periodic basis, and they should be asked to leave if it becomes clear that they have little or no growth potential.

Group IV: Anchor Tenants

Anchor Tenants are admitted to the incubator for two reasons: (1) they help provide a stable cash flow to the incubator, and (2) they have one or more business reasons for being in close proximity to other companies in the incubator. For example, they may be able to provide services to incubator companies (e.g., a Small Business Development Center), or they may want to develop incubator companies as clients (e.g., legal, accounting or marketing firms).

Regardless of whether they are relatively large firms or one- or two-person service providers, Anchor Tenants should understand that they will not receive proactive assistance from the incubator president.

A USEFUL ANCHOR TENANT

A small technical writing firm applied to the incubator because the incubator sponsor was one of its primary customers. The company was mature and financially capable of paying its bills. In addition, its services could be useful to other incubator companies who needed help developing promotional materials and manuals. The incubator president accepted the company into the incubator but provided no assistance other than an occasional referral to a potential customer.

STATE AGENCY AS AN ANCHOR TENANT

One incubator sponsored by a Chamber of Commerce started out with a part-time incubator president who was a loaned executive from the Chamber. In order to enhance the incubator's capacity for on-site counseling and mentoring, a state agency with a mandate to provide business assistance to the community was accepted as an anchor tenant. This arrangement was a source of steady revenue to the incubator, helped the state agency fulfill its mission and enabled the incubator companies to gain easy access to more services than the incubator staff could provide.

Once the incubator firms have been segmented according to this evaluation framework, the Group II firms (the Up-and-Comers) should be re-examined and ranked according to the potential competitive advantages and the offsetting competitive disadvantages. Some of the companies in the group may warrant aggressive, proactive intervention assistance from the president; the rest, while still holding significant promise, may need to be linked to resources outside the incubator.

As noted above, the assignment of companies to one of these four groups—based on the assessment of their needs, their growth potential, and their stage of development—is an important part of the admissions process. Each company's management team and the incubator president should periodically review the progress of the company and the effectiveness of the incubator's assistance efforts. These discussions can reveal whether the current types of assistance being provided should be maintained, enhanced or discontinued.

In a dynamic and successful best practices incubator, Group I: Superstar companies will be graduating; some Group II: Up-and-Comer companies will thrive and develop into Group I companies; new Group II companies will emerge from the pool of current Group III: Long Shot companies; and Group IV: Anchor Tenants will help stabilize the resource base and will provide services to tenants.

The following action steps summarize how to establish an effective recruitment and selection process.

ACTION STEPS

FOR ESTABLISHING AN EFFECTIVE
RECRUITING AND SELECTION PROCESS

1. Develop a marketing capacity that builds on the market awareness established during the feasibility study stage. Depend as much as possible on board members, a board committee, other stakeholder volunteers and the incubator business manager. Minimize the involvement of the incubator president.

2. Structure an admissions process that involves volunteers and the incubator business manager in the information exchange and pre-screening phases. Engage the incubator president only when the prospective company has a high probability of being a good applicant. Minimize the expenditure of time and resources to get to the decision point.

3. Develop and apply admissions criteria that reflect the principles of successful business incubation, i.e., that provide a revenue-generating capacity to allow the incubator to operate like a business within the financial model adopted at start-up and fulfill the mandate to assist companies with high growth potential.

4. Achieve the desirable outcomes of the admissions process: (1) establish clear expectations for company and incubator performance, (2) reach a decision regarding which segment the company is in, and (3) reach agreement with the entrepreneur regarding what each party must commit to delivering.

9

Making the Difference: Serving Client Needs

The recurring theme of this book is that the ultimate purpose of an incubator is to enhance the start-up, survival, growth and success rate of new ventures. The incubator management team provides various types of assistance in order to achieve this objective.

A best-practices incubator president must:

- have considerable knowledge and understanding of the problems that start-up companies experience
- develop a "portfolio" of programs and services appropriate for the kinds of companies that are likely to locate in the incubator
- be able to assess the strengths and weaknesses of each company in the incubator
- develop individualized and tailored programs of assistance for each company to enable the entrepreneur and team to capitalize on strengths and correct weaknesses

BEST PRACTICE #9:

CUSTOMIZE THE DELIVERY OF ASSISTANCE AND ADDRESS THE DEVELOPMENTAL NEEDS OF EACH COMPANY.

This chapter describes assistance mechanisms that are utilized by the most successful incubator programs and delineates how they can be implemented to achieve maximum impact.

The development of a "portfolio" of programs and services is very important; "one size" does not fit all companies. Indeed, the development of a specific program of assistance for each company, with goals and deadlines that the entrepreneur and incubator president agree to, is part of the value the incubator can add to the company.

The eight best practices discussed thus far create the foundation for the ninth best practice. The remainder of this chapter details the following action steps for growing companies.

Steps for Growing Companies

1. Understand the common deficiencies of incubator companies.

2. Segment the population of incubator companies.

3. Develop a complete portfolio of assistance mechanisms.

4. Customize the delivery of assistance to each segment of the incubator population and to each individual company within those segments.

5. Move companies through the assistance process and toward graduation from the incubator.

COMMON DEFICIENCIES OF INCUBATOR COMPANIES

Most entrepreneurs launching new ventures have significant deficiencies with respect to the resources and talents necessary for success. Some of the common deficiencies faced by start-ups are reflected in the list below.

Product or Service
- Entrepreneurs often focus far too long on perfecting the invention, product, service or prototype and run out of time and money before they get to market.
- Entrepreneurs seldom do market research and tend to assume that they know what the customer wants in the product or service.
- Entrepreneurs seldom test products for manufacturability and typically have no capacity and no plan for manufacturing the product.
- Entrepreneurs often have not determined whether their product or service can be delivered at a profit.

Cash Flow
- Some entrepreneurs believe negative cash flow will turn positive, but few have a plan to make this happen. Some do not even understand the concept of cash flow.
- Entrepreneurs typically have inadequate financial management skills.
- Entrepreneurs seldom know what sources of funds to tap or strategies to use in order to get more cash when needed.
- Entrepreneurs too often assume customers will make prompt payment for goods and services.

Sales and Marketing

- Entrepreneurs tend to underestimate the importance of sales.
- Entrepreneurs seldom comprehend the importance of market position.
- Entrepreneurs usually have difficulty assessing the competition.
- Entrepreneurs frequently underestimate the time it takes to get the product to market.

The Entrepreneurial Team

- Entrepreneurs tend to overestimate their personal capacity and do not understand their strengths and weaknesses.
- Entrepreneurs do not know how to recruit and select the people needed to fill out the management team.
- Entrepreneurs undervalue complementary talent, are unwilling to allocate adequate resources to acquiring talent, and often end up getting what they paid for—marginal or inadequate performers.
- Entrepreneurs do not recognize the importance of interpersonal relationships among the members of the management team and do not understand how to work to create an effective team.

NO SALES = NO CASH = NO COMPANY

A new spin-off of a successful regional company was launched by three engineers. In the business plan for the new firm, completion of the prototype was predicted to require three months. The financial *pro formas* indicated that the company would have over $1 million in revenues during the ensuing six months. During the admissions process, the incubator president stated that he believed the three founders could achieve prototype completion in three months but achieving the revenue goal would be much more difficult. His assessment turned out to be accurate. During a performance review at the nine-month mark, at which point revenues still stood at zero, one of the entrepreneurs said to the incubator president, "We heard your advice nine months ago about the challenge of selling but really didn't understand. Now after six months of working hard and having nothing to show for it, we appreciate your warning." The company never completed a single sale and within a year was out of business.

Deficiencies will vary from company to company, but discerning that variability and developing plans to address such deficiencies is the mark of a good incubator president. For example, in a situation where the company has a high rate of negative cash flow, the entrepreneur may not have time to develop financial management skills; hence, the company will have to hire a full-time or part-time chief financial officer. On the other hand, a new venture with marginal but positive cash flow may be able to grow slowly, thus enabling the founders to develop the knowledge and skills necessary to grow the company.

In these two situations, the overall critical success factor for each firm is the same: managing cash flow. However, the techniques for addressing this factor vary dramatically, and the incubator president will have to develop two entirely different plans. In the first situation, the incubator president will need to help the company identify and attract talent and the capital to pay for it. For the second situation, the president will mentor the entrepreneur and the team; direct them to others who can assist with their growth and development; and alert them to programs especially designed to teach skills in financial management and organization development.

A best-practices incubator president will know that:

1. a new venture must have or must develop an entrepreneur or entrepreneurial team with the skills and experience necessary to grow the company
2. a venture must have a product or service to sell
3. there must be a market for the product or service, or the entrepreneur must be able to create a new market
4. the venture must have access to capital or its equivalent to survive periods of negative cash flow

As noted earlier, most ventures start with weaknesses or deficiencies in one or more of these areas—which must be addressed before the cash runs out. In many cases, an entrepreneur's relative strength in one area can provide a competitive advantage that may compensate, up to a point, for relative weakness in another area. However, some minimum level of development in all four areas is necessary if a venture is to survive and succeed.

Although new ventures are vulnerable and can fail even if they do all the right things, the probability of their success is related to the entrepreneur's maturity vis-à-vis recognizing and developing a plan to compensate for his/her deficiencies. Incubators can provide temporary resources to help compensate for deficiencies in the short term. But in the long run, the incubator president must help entrepreneurs figure out their strengths and weaknesses and develop plans to capitalize on the former and eliminate the latter.

SEGMENT THE POPULATION

The incubator president needs to employ the same segmentation grid described in the last chapter and categorize companies according to Long Shots, Up-and-Comers, Superstars, and Anchor Tenants. He/she then needs to allocate time and resources to help each company achieve its plan and grow as quickly as possible. The incubator president also needs to monitor the incubator companies and regularly assess their progress and development. Over time, companies may be reassigned to different quadrants of the segmentation grid and a modified assistance program developed to meet their new status. For example, Long Shot companies may progress to the point where they become Up-and-Comers; if not, they need to "graduate" from the incubator to make room for new tenant companies with greater potential. Similarly Up-and-Comers will ideally mature into Superstars. If not, they may be reassigned to the Long Shot category or be asked to leave the incubator to make way for a new generation of companies. At some point Superstars will literally outgrow the incubator, both physically and psychologically.

DEVELOP A PORTFOLIO OF ASSISTANCE MECHANISMS

While a start-up incubator may have limited capacity to provide assistance to its companies, a best practices incubator president will continually strive to expand and refine the incubator's programs and services. Just as the entrepreneur needs to be realistic about his/her own capabilities and skills and what the company can deliver, the incubator president needs to be realistic when assessing what the incubator has to offer client companies. A typical inventory of resources might include:

1. the knowledge, skills and experience of the incubator president and the rest of the incubator staff
2. the proximity to other entrepreneurs from whom entrepreneurs learn and gain skills
3. the business assistance programs and financial resources of the community that can be accessed through the incubator network
4. the knowledge, skills and experience of the know-how network, including the boards of directors or advisers of the incubator, which can be accessed to help companies on an "as needed" basis
5. the resources and expertise that may be available through the "extended" network of the incubator and its community supporters, contacts and companies in other cities, states, even countries
6. the physical facility, conference rooms, library and business services in the incubator

In order to successfully connect these resources to client companies, the incubator president needs to make the descriptions of the incubator assistance and services as concrete as possible. Specific services or "packages" of assistance need to be defined and described in printed materials that can be shared with tenant companies and distributed as part of the marketing materials.

After assessing the needs and capacities of the entrepreneur and the firm and determining the resources and expertise available through the incubator, the incubator president can develop a plan which outlines a program of assistance specifically designed to meet the needs of each company. Each plan should identify three ways of delivering assistance.

Counseling of Entrepreneurs by the Incubator President

Most incubator presidents see counseling of entrepreneurs as one of their

Three Ways of Delivering Assistance

1. **Counseling**—of the entrepreneurs by the incubator president and/or the incubator staff

2. **Connecting**—of entrepreneurs by the incubator president to resources and expertise inside and outside the incubator

3. **Creating the Culture**—of the incubator. Creating the incubator culture or environment includes provision of facilities and shared business services, co-location of entrepreneurs who can benefit from networking with each other, training and education programs and the broad spectrum of assistance that facilitates the development of new ventures

primary roles, and entrepreneurs often comment positively on the value of their incubator president as a sounding board and adviser. In addition, entrepreneurs frequently mention the emotional support, counsel and advice the incubator president provides, as well as referrals to resources in the community.

ROLE OF THE PRESIDENT

A founder and president of one incubator company spoke for many incubator entrepreneurs when he described his incubator president as "somewhere between a father figure and a business adviser."

Counseling usually begins during the admissions process, when the incubator president or staff review the business plan of the entrepreneur and provide feedback about what's needed to improve the plan. Assistance in developing a business plan is the most common form of counseling cited by entrepreneurs, followed by counseling related to team building, financial management, marketing and gaining access to capital. However, experience suggests that there is significant room for improvement in the counseling of incubator client companies. Both incubator presidents and their entrepreneurs have suggested that achieving best practice in counseling requires special attention to the following two factors:

1. Specificity of advice
2. Follow-through and persistence

Specificity of Advice
The general advice that a competent incubator president provides can

make a significant difference in the rate of development of most incubator companies. However, at some point even the most competent incubator president will simply not have the knowledge and experience to move beyond the general advice that is applicable to most ventures and to provide advice that is specific to the characteristics and unique needs of a particular venture.

The challenge for each incubator president is to counsel an incubator company through the stage where his/her advice can be helpful and prepare the company to access the more specific expertise it requires as it matures. That means developing the capacities of the current members of the management team, forming a strong and competent board of directors, using outside consultants when needed and acquiring additional management talent if necessary to compensate for deficiencies.

Follow-Through and Persistence

There are many demands on the time and attention of the incubator president, and the time that is available for counseling is usually spread across many client companies. As a result, incubator presidents often fail to muster sufficient intensity and continuity in the counseling process, and thus their impact is limited. In a best practices incubator, the program will be structured to ensure sufficient intensity and follow-through in the counseling efforts of the president so as to achieve the desired impact. Persistence and follow-through require great discipline on the part of the incubator president. Failure to sustain that discipline will often allow marginal firms to slide into failure, instead of being propelled toward success.

THE INCUBATOR PRESIDENT MUST PERSIST

An incubator president was very enthusiastic about the prospects for one of his client companies but felt that the company was wasting valuable time and resources in constantly revising and perfecting its product, rather than completing a prototype and connecting with potential customers. The incubator president had repeatedly met with the company principals to get them to focus on the marketplace, but his efforts met with little success. He grew frustrated with the company and turned his attention to other companies that were more responsive to his advice. One of the company principals expressed disappointment that the incubator president had not been more persistent in his efforts to force the company to address marketing issues. Although the company eventually overcame its difficulties, had the incubator president persisted with his counseling, the company might have been able to ramp-up more quickly.

This need for persistence, intensity and follow-through is evident in the case of another incubator president and entrepreneur.

PERSISTENT AND INTENSE COUNSELING

Even though the counseling relationship with their incubator president
had been positive overall, the company principals had four years of marginal success and many setbacks that kept them in a financially vulnerable position. Both the incubator president and the entrepreneurs
acknowledged that the lack of intensity and persistence in the counseling efforts left the entrepreneurs to struggle up their learning curve more
slowly than they might have if a best practice counseling effort had been
part of their incubator experience. When asked how the incubator could
have been more effective, one of the principals commented: "A more
continuous and consistent counseling process to make us wiser, faster."

Personal counseling and support in response to short-term needs are necessary but not sufficient. Incubator presidents must also provide intensive,
specific business counseling that extends over a period of time and is related to the company's developmental plan. Specific suggestions for improving
performance with respect to counseling of incubator companies include the
key concepts outlined in Figure 18.

Connecting Entrepreneurs to External Resources

When the incubator president does not have enough specific knowledge
or resources to meet the unique needs of a particular incubator company,
then he/she should turn to experts in the community network. Community
leaders and business service professionals are often willing to provide access
to services pro bono or at discounted rates, as a public service or as a long-
term business-development activity.

WHY OTHERS PROVIDE PRO BONO SERVICES

A major accounting firm provided services to a promising incubator
start-up company at no charge through its emerging business services
division. The company grew rapidly enough to be ranked among the top
firms on the *Inc.* magazine list of 500 fastest-growing small companies
in America. In early 1994 the company went public. The accounting
firm generated substantial fees for its participation in the initial public
offering process and has successfully retained the company as a major
client.

Connecting client companies to the know-how network also allows the
incubator president to leverage his/her time. This network can be used to
gain access to legal, accounting, insurance, financing and other types of
business expertise. In addition networking is used to access specialized
facilities, laboratories and equipment that may be available through affiliation with a sponsoring institution such as a university or an economic
development entity.

FIGURE 18

Key Concepts of Successful Counseling

1. Take time for reactive counseling that responds to the crisis or problem of the moment, but also...

2. Schedule time for proactive, extended counseling designed to push the incubator company up its growth and maturation curve.

3. Make the tough choices regarding which ventures can benefit the most from the assistance and counseling the incubator president can provide. After making those choices, then provide the persistent, intense counseling to those companies to move them up their growth curves.

4. For the Up-and-Comer companies, think of counseling in terms of phases:

   • the admissions and entry phase
   • intensive counseling by the incubator president and preparation for transfer to external advisers
   • transfer counseling activities to a carefully selected board of advisers or consultants

5. Use the external know-how network to leverage the counseling capacity of the incubator program staff.

THE IMPORTANCE OF A KNOW-HOW NETWORK

The president and founder of a company located in a western incubator was in the middle of a project when a patent-infringement allegation appeared. There was tremendous pressure to move quickly. The entrepreneur had never worked with an attorney on general legal issues, much less patent litigation. He presented his problem to his incubator president, and within a half hour the incubator president had arranged an appointment for that afternoon with a local patent attorney. Within 24 hours the appropriate letters had been drafted and mailed to resolve the situation.

Connecting Entrepreneurs to Financing

Providing access to sources of debt and equity financing is a special type of networking. Venture financing is consistently listed as the biggest challenge facing incubator presidents and their client companies. Incubator presidents play a valuable role in counseling entrepreneurs about the requirements, attitudes and expectations of investors and the advantages and disadvantages of alternative sources of financing. Most ventures in an incubator do not have sufficient assets to qualify for traditional collateral-based lending or for working-capital loans. Exceptionally promising ventures may qualify for equity financing, and some may be able to tap into federal, state, regional or local economic development agency lending programs. Many incubators have connected their client companies to these sorts of programs. Some incubators have even developed their own affiliated financing entities.

Networking Challenges

While there are many potential advantages to using the incubator network, there are also potential downsides to networking that must be guarded against if the process is going to have the desired impact:

- inadequacy of the network contact
- unresponsiveness of the entrepreneur
- lack of follow-through by the incubator president
- the investment of time required to develop, cultivate and sustain the know-how network

Inadequacy of the Network Contact

Both the entrepreneur and the network contact or expert will be frustrated if the person to whom the entrepreneur has been referred does not have the knowledge or experience to deal directly with the problem at hand. For example, a general business attorney will seldom be able to help with intellectual property problems. A tax accountant will not likely be able to provide adequate answers about securities law. The incubator president needs to know what each expert in the know-how network can and cannot deliver and make certain that the person has the expertise to help the entrepreneur address the core problem.

The incubator president needs to prepare the entrepreneur to ask what time and resources the expert is willing to commit and what compensation is expected. If the experts are not fully committed to working with and resolving the problems of the entrepreneurs and if the entrepreneurs do not know what questions to ask or how to make the most of the know-how network, then the network will add little value to the incubator companies.

Unresponsiveness of the Entrepreneur

Sometimes the entrepreneur does not have the capacity or willingness to respond to the advice of the network expert.

POOR USE OF KNOW-HOW NETWORK

One entrepreneur joined an incubator specifically to tap into the incubator's access to outside experts who could help him develop a system for financial record keeping. The incubator president contacted a senior partner of a major accounting firm and an accounting professor from a local business college to help the entrepreneur. However, the entrepreneur's interest in developing new components for old personal computers overshadowed his interest in developing financial systems for his business. He failed to spend time working with his know-how network experts and missed many meetings with them. Finally, the accountant and the accounting professor were unwilling to invest any more time in the entrepreneur because of his unresponsiveness. Shortly thereafter the entrepreneur left the incubator and returned to his electronics shop in the basement of his parents' home.

Sometimes an incubator president needs to invest the time and energy to help an entrepreneur develop the capacity to respond to assistance. If the entrepreneur is unwilling to respond, the incubator president needs to determine why. That may mean helping the entrepreneur to understand the value of what is being offered and to develop more openness to assistance and an enhanced responsiveness. Other times it means facilitating an efficient disconnect.

Lack of Follow-Through by the Incubator President

In the ideal world the incubator president will correctly diagnose the problem, connect the entrepreneur to the appropriate expert in the know-how network and then leave them to resolve the problem. However, in the real world the entrepreneur and the expert usually need the incubator president to check whether the expert is really providing advice in a form and manner the entrepreneur is able to accept and whether the entrepreneur is implementing the advice. The incubator president needs to follow through and complete the feedback loop, providing reinforcement as needed.

The Investment of Time Required to Develop, Cultivate and Sustain the Know-How Network

Without appropriate direction and management, a know-how network can take on a life of its own, requiring a large, continuing effort to sustain it. In addition, members of the network need to be motivated to have a positive impact on the incubator companies. Sometimes service professionals just want to be able to say they are affiliated with a highly visible business incubator; others may be looking for an entree into the incubator network and affiliation with other service professionals. Sustaining an extended and largely unproductive network can significantly diminish the capacity of the incubator president to provide effective business assistance.

HELPING COMPANIES VS. SUSTAINING THE NETWORK

A highly recognized veteran incubator president captured the frustration related to investing time in sustaining the know-how network: "My worst fault is not giving my entrepreneurs enough time because there are too many networking meetings that I feel I must attend. Time is my worst problem. I just don't have enough of it."

The goal of the incubator president with respect to developing the know-how network should be to identify and manage the core group of experts who have the competencies to resolve most problems faced by the incubator companies—as efficiently and effectively as possible. As noted earlier, directors of the incubator board or other stakeholder champions should be responsible for sustaining and managing the extended know-how network, the second tier of know-how experts. The key concepts of successful networking are presented in Figure 19.

Creating the Incubator Environment

Experience suggests that creating the right kind of "user friendly" environment in the incubator can have a positive impact on survival rates of new ventures. The key elements of this environment include:

- shared facilities and services
- enhanced opportunities for entrepreneur-to-entrepreneur networking
- training and educational programs

Shared Facilities and Services

The environment of a business incubator is designed to enable start-up companies to accelerate their development and model their behavior after companies that are more developed—before they run out of cash. The classic romantic tale of starting up a future entrepreneurial super success in the entrepreneur's garage needs to be tempered by the reality of a lonely struggle for existence in a barren environment. By comparison, the start-up company that locates in an incubator will have most of the amenities of an established company, including (1) shared business services (telephone answering, word processing, and receptionist); (2) access to a professional-looking conference room; and (3) office equipment (e.g., copier, fax machine, report binding machine, computers). In addition, these facilities and resources are provided at a reasonable rate, under a flexible lease agreement and by a friendly landlord prepared to accommodate the changing needs of incubator companies.

The benefits are obvious and quantifiable. The incubator companies are able to conserve cash, to avoid long-term financial commitments and yet have access to professional business services that can speed them along their growth curve. By conserving cash the firms are able to increase the probability that they will survive the start-up phase of their development.

FIGURE 19

Key Concepts of Successful Networking

1. Identify the needs of client companies that the incubator president is unable to address.

2. Make sure the network expert to whom the client company is referred has the required expertise and is willing to commit the time necessary to get the job done. Follow up to make sure the connection was productive.

3. Invest time in helping the entrepreneurs develop the capacity to make effective use of experts and service professionals.

4. Minimize the time required for the care and feeding of the know-how network.

5. Recognize that a small core group of committed and capable professionals will generally be much more productive than a large and uncommitted group.

6. Encourage members of the board to cultivate experts within the extended know-how network who can provide the specialized expertise that entrepreneurs in the incubator may need which may not be available through the core group of experts.

And while flexible lease space and shared business services are very important, the credibility and visibility the incubator provides may be even more important.

INCUBATOR PROVIDES CREDIBILITY TO TENANTS

A veteran business manager for a large national department store started his own electrical-products distributor. Although he survived for several years, his growth was limited by lack of working capital. When a local business incubator was developed, he was one of the first entrepreneurs to be accepted. The entrepreneur was able to leverage the tremendous visibility and public support generated by the start-up of the incubator to gain the attention of the local banking community. With a working-capital line of credit, his firm grew from approximately $1 million to $7 million annually within six years.

Networking Among Entrepreneurs

The impact of co-locating entrepreneurs in a business incubator has been well documented. First and foremost they learn from each other, buy and sell products and services to each other, sometimes share customers and suppliers and often share the emotional ups and downs of starting up a new venture.

The value of networking with other entrepreneurs is reflected in the comments of the president of an incubator company:

THE VALUE OF CAMARADERIE

"One of the greatest benefits of being in the incubator is being part of what we call the 'Sixth Floor Mafia'—the group of lean and mean companies that share their dry ice, their machine shop, their knowledge and their problems. Some questions are best answered by people who have just gone through a similar experience."

Much of this networking among entrepreneurs happens spontaneously as they meet in the hallways of the incubator, but there are some things that can be done to enhance this process. Although most incubators need to minimize the amount of common space that is not revenue-producing, creating a few common areas that foster interaction can be a real plus.

DESIGNING THE INCUBATOR FOR INTERACTIONS

At one incubator center, all the common-use equipment (fax, copier, typewriter) and the company mailboxes are located in the lunch room, with a coffee pot, a microwave, a refrigerator and a sink. The development of a "community room" has significantly enhanced the relationships among entrepreneurs in the incubator.

Training and Educational Programs

Many, if not most, entrepreneurs lack basic business experience, skills and knowledge. Incubator presidents can help ameliorate these deficiencies by organizing an ongoing series of training and educational programs, which become part of the "standard package" available to all incubator companies. Commonly structured in short-course format (e.g., offered at breakfast, during a brown bag lunch, or in short, half-day seminars), such programs can provide general information on a variety of topics: sales/marketing, financial management, intellectual property, management information systems, accessing capital and team building. This is a quick way for client companies to learn the basic language and concepts of business.

Often the greatest challenge in achieving impact is stimulating and then sustaining the participation of the incubator entrepreneurs. Three strategies are recommended: (1) make it clear during the admissions process that entrepreneurs are expected to participate in the training and educational activities of the incubator; (2) create a system to notify entrepreneurs of programs and specify the merits of participating; and (3) encourage the leaders among the client companies to lead by example and to encourage the other entrepreneurs and members of their teams to participate.

The benefits of training and educational programs include:

- transfer of information and skills to entrepreneurs, which may be particularly important for Long Shot entrepreneurs with prospects for moving up to Up-and-Comer status
- opportunities for entrepreneurs within and outside the incubator to network and become familiar with each other's products and services
- forum to promote additional connections between entrepreneurs and experts in the know-how network
- outreach to the local entrepreneurial community as a way to market the incubator and identify prospective incubator clients

CUSTOMIZE THE DELIVERY OF ASSISTANCE

Business incubator presidents play three very important roles: (1) they provide personal and professional counseling on a short-term and a long-term basis, (2) they connect entrepreneurs to other experts who provide on-the-spot or long-term counseling and to other resources the companies need but don't have, and (3) they create an environment conducive to business incubation. As the practice of business incubation evolves, it is becoming clear that one of the great challenges for incubator presidents is to custom-tailor assistance to meet the needs of each client company and determine the time frame within which the assistance will be provided.

The Reactive vs. Proactive Approach to Providing Assistance

In the reactive approach the incubator president provides assistance only when asked to do so by an entrepreneur. There are a number of positive aspects to this approach. It fosters an openness and collegiality that encourages entrepreneurs to come to the incubator president with their problems and concerns. If the entrepreneur is taking the initiative and the time to query the incubator president, then it is reasonable to expect that he/she is likely to accept and implement that advice. This approach is particularly appropriate for Long Shot companies and may also be used with Superstars and Anchor Tenants.

REACTIVE APPROACH TO COUNSELING

The current standard approach to counseling appears to be largely reactive, as reflected in the comments of one incubator president: "I came out of the consulting field, where I was accustomed to giving advice on all kinds of matters, from financing to engineering. But in the incubator environment, I quickly found that what the entrepreneurs wanted was someone with whom to talk out their problems: They wanted me to listen, to be a sounding board. So I just ask open-ended questions like, 'Did you think of this?' 'Why did you do that?' After our conversations, about 90 percent of them go away having solved their own problems."

The reactive approach requires the entrepreneur to take the initiative to seek assistance. It also requires the incubator president to play a Socratic role and ask the kinds of questions that will cause the entrepreneur to recognize problems and devise solutions.

The problem with this approach is that most entrepreneurs wait to seek assistance until they are faced with a crisis, when they need too much assistance in too little time to allow effective intervention. While the entrepreneur and incubator president may be able to solve the immediate problem, that short-term success may do little to support the kinds of change required in order for the venture to grow and develop. Unless the president helps the entrepreneur to focus on the strategic issues related to critical success factors, reactive intervention is unlikely to have a long-term impact on the success of the venture. For this reason the reactive approach alone will be insufficient for the Up-and-Comer companies that require intensive, persistent assistance.

Best-practices incubator presidents take a proactive approach to providing assistance, especially with Up-and-Comer companies—from the time these companies are admitted to the incubator. The development of a plan of assistance is the first signal that the incubator president intends to play a proactive role with client companies. But, as one incubator company entrepreneur noted, it is not easy to be proactive:

WHY PRESIDENTS MUST BE PROACTIVE

"Incubator presidents try to help companies, but they often meet with apathy from the entrepreneurs. Some of them just give up and retreat to a facilities-management role. But they need to persevere and keep pushing the entrepreneurs to take advantage of the incubator programs. There's a bigger picture and part of the president's job is to keep reminding people of the bigger picture. It is easy to ignore this when you're trying to survive in the short term."

Many incubator companies have no boards of directors, and their management teams are generally incomplete. By providing proactive assistance, incubator presidents can play a valuable transitional role and help compensate for these deficiencies.

WHY PRESIDENTS MUST CHALLENGE COMPANIES

The need for the proactive approach is evident in the commentary of another incubator company founder: "One thing that could be provided is a critique, a real honest critique, a business critique of where we are going. What are we doing? Are we floundering? Why are we floundering? A company that locates in an incubator ought to be subjected to some review, and I don't mean just superficial review. Many boards of directors are very distant or just don't have enough knowledge. The incubator president needs to play the role of board director and know the details of what's happening and why. This kind of intensive review could be painful, and it is not necessarily pleasant, but it is essential if we're going to grow up and develop."

The proactive assistance effort can take two other forms. The incubator president might become a quasi-member of the management team until someone with the necessary skills and expertise can be recruited. Alternatively, the incubator president can help identify a team of experts who can serve as a board of advisers and work with the entrepreneur.

MOVE COMPANIES TOWARD GRADUATION

As noted earlier, the incubator president will not generally have time to provide intensive, proactive assistance to all the companies in the incubator. Instead, this type of assistance should be reserved for a manageable number of the Up-and-Comer companies. For example, if the incubator president commits 50% time to this effort and expects to dedicate approximately a half day per week to each company, only four to six companies can be served at a time. Therefore the incubator president needs to become intensively involved in moving these Up-and-Comer companies from the marginal, survival start-up mode to being firmly established on the road to success as quickly as possible.

If all goes according to plan, Up-and-Comer companies will mature to the point of "graduating" from the intensive, proactive assistance program provided by the incubator. There are a number of possible successful outcomes. An Up-and-Comer company may move up to the Superstar category, it may stabilize as a small but successful business or it may be ready to merge with or be acquired by another company. However, in some cases, the company may not mature according to plan and may drift back into the Long Shot category, leave the incubator, quietly go out of business or, in rare cases, fail spectacularly. Whatever the outcome, the Up-and-Comer company participating in an intensive proactive assistance program will more than likely soon leave the incubator. The "graduation" will permit the incubator president to identify the next most promising Up-and-Comer from the portfolio of incubator companies and to admit that company into the proactive assistance program.

ONE OF MANY GRADUATION ALTERNATIVES

The incubator president and client company founders agreed that the company needed a new CEO in order to grow and develop, so they made this part of the plan. With the help of the incubator president, the company president hired someone from the know-how network who had been advising him as a part-time chief executive officer. Within six months the new CEO helped the three founding members of the entrepreneurial team recognize that their real strengths and interests were in software development, not building and managing a new venture. The CEO helped the company "graduate" by identifying a corporate partner and negotiating the transition from independent venture in the incubator to captive software development team operating within the corporate partner.

As a company matures from an Up-and-Comer into a Superstar, it will typically acquire sufficient internal management capacity to supplant the role the incubator president has played. The quasi-board of directors or advisers should then be replaced by an effective, professional, permanent board of directors. Under ideal circumstances, this transformation can take place over six to twelve months.

THE STORY OF A SUCCESSFUL ASSISTANCE PROGRAM

One incubator company, barely squeaking by financially, had a "lone ranger" entrepreneur with a habit of hiring marginal employees. He had a tendency to focus on internal operations and inappropriately equated simple networking with a professional sales and marketing effort. The incubator president succeeded in convincing the entrepreneur to hire employees capable of taking on most of the responsibility for operations. In addition, the entrepreneur gained an appreciation for the difference between networking and aggressive marketing. At the end of six months, the entrepreneur had begun to learn how to use his board of directors and had a more competent venture team and a commitment to marketing. The intensive, proactive assistance served as a catalyst for the growth of the entrepreneur and his venture. The company tripled its revenues and number of employees in three years and expanded its geographic market from the state to the national level.

The following action steps will increase the effectiveness of incubator assistance programs.

ACTION STEPS

FOR INCREASING THE EFFECTIVENESS OF
INCUBATOR ASSISTANCE PROGRAMS

1. Maximize the time of the incubator president available for proactive assistance. Other activities that require the time of the president need to be minimized (e.g., governance) or off-loaded to other staff, to members of the board or to volunteers (e.g., managing the incubator facility, incubator operations, managing the extended know-how network).

2. Dedicate the time required to achieve a success threshold. Use intensity and persistence when working with chosen companies. The incubator president will need to dedicate more time to fewer companies. This requires the president to make tough decisions about which companies will be chosen for the proactive assistance process and which companies will receive less intensive help through the know-how network.

3. Increase the specificity of assistance. The incubator president needs to call on others, including experts from the know-how network, who can provide the advice and resources required to address the specific needs of each company.

4. Increase the capacity of both the entrepreneurs and the incubator president to be effective participants in the proactive assistance process. The incubator president must pick and choose those entrepreneurs for whom proactive assistance will be the catalyst for a significant company transformation. The incubator president should help the entrepreneurs develop their entrepreneurial capacities. By the same token, the board members of the incubator must select a president who will provide this kind of assistance if they are going to achieve the first principle of business incubation—focus on helping companies grow and develop. The board should expect the incubator president to develop effective business skills and provide the resources and opportunities for that to occur.

10

Beyond Incubators: Emerging Trends & Strategies for Business Incubation

Like entrepreneurs trying to grow companies, those responsible for incubation programs must engage in periodic and systematic assessment, i.e., assess the incubator's strengths and weaknesses, how it is changing over time and to what extent the needs of the client companies are being addressed. At minimum the president and board members need to measure progress against plan or toward achievement of specific goals. Ideally they will measure the incubator's achievements against a standard or benchmark. The set of principles and practices outlined in this book provide such a yardstick against which to evaluate current practice. However, regardless of whether internal or external measures and standards are used, a best practices incubator's operations, programs and services will be evaluated at regular intervals.

Best Practice #10:

ENGAGE IN CONTINUAL EVALUATION AND IMPROVEMENT AS THE INCUBATOR PROGRESSES THROUGH VARIOUS STAGES OF DEVELOPMENT AND AS THE NEEDS OF CLIENT COMPANIES CHANGE OVER TIME.

This book has provided standards against which to measure the performance of incubator programs and guidelines for continuous improvement. However, it does not provide a detailed evaluation methodology. The Economic Development Administration of the U.S. Department of Commerce and the National Business Incubation Association (NBIA) have invested considerable funds and time in collaborating on the development of an evaluation methodology handbook entitled: *The Evaluation of Business Incubation Projects: A Comprehensive Manual.*

Rather than summarize that manual here, we direct the reader to contact NBIA for more information about how to secure a copy of this manual.

A list of this and other useful references concerning business incubation, entrepreneurship and venture financing can be found in the "Further Readings" section. The point is, incubators need to evaluate their operations and performance on a regular basis.

One of the marks of an entrepreneur is the individual drive and creativity in navigating through the risks, uncertainties and setbacks toward success. Similarly, the sponsors, stakeholders and president of each individual incubator will need to chart their own course toward best practices. The principles and practices outlined in this book are not hard and fast rules. Instead they provide a structure to achieve a vision—this vision, described below, is from the perspective of an incubator team that has established itself as a successful catalyst for growing new ventures and creating new jobs.

VISION OF A BEST-PRACTICES INCUBATOR

A feasibility study verified the opportunity to meet the needs of the entrepreneurial marketplace with the capacities of an incubator and the availability of financial and other resources required to establish an incubator program. The business plan and financial model defined what would be required to make the incubator self-sustainable. The incubator project attracted a champion and the required financial investment. Its sponsors recognized that it would take three to five years for the incubator to become self-sustainable and made the necessary "investment" after completing "due diligence" investigations with the conviction that they would achieve a satisfactory "return on investment."

The incubator has been structured with a working board that provides assistance to the incubator and to client companies, with minimal time spent on governance activities. Stakeholders are engaged selectively to provide assistance to the incubator and the companies. Board members and/or staff take care of the facilities and manages the "nuts and bolts" aspects of the incubator's business operations. The incubator president has been selected for his/her capacity to help entrepreneurs and focuses on that task, spending as much time as possible, 50% or more, working with companies and helping the entrepreneurs move their companies through the early and difficult stages of development.

The board, the incubator president and client companies all understand that because the incubator accepts, works with and adds value to companies during their high risk, start-up stage, there should be some pay-back, some way the incubator can share in the future revenue stream and/or increased value of the client companies downstream. Consequently, not only do companies pay rent and fees for leased space and shared services, but they also compensate the incubator for strategic business assistance in cash, equity and/or royalties.

The incubator building was selected to enable the incubator to achieve financial self-sustainability and to provide an environment conducive for development of entrepreneurs and their companies. Rather than marketing the incubator as a low-rent, low-cost facility, the board and president market access to a "success" environment and to people, programs and services that will help a company get a "jump-start" on success.

Four types of companies or organizations comprise the mix of clients.

1. *"Up-and-Comers"—companies that show significant signs of promise and, with intensive and persistent assistance from the incubator president and others, may well become growing successful companies*
2. *"Superstars"— successful, fast-growing companies that are getting ready to graduate from the incubator and that can still benefit from selective and strategic assistance from the incubator*
3. *"Long Shots"—companies that benefit by just being located in the incubator and can pay rent but are not far enough along in their development to deserve much time or attention from the incubator president*
4. *"Anchor Tenants"—Established companies, government agencies or service organizations that benefit by being in the incubator and being close to potential clients (start-up companies) located in the incubator or serviced by the incubator. They pay premium rent but require little time or attention from the incubator president.*

Finally, the person chosen as incubator president knows enough about the process of entrepreneurship and company growth to be able to analyze the strengths and weaknesses of each company. Recognizing that a good president will spot emerging problems before the entrepreneur encounters them, he/she develops a resource bank of people, programs and services that enables him/her to custom-tailor assistance to a particular company's needs and stage of development. This best practices incubator president is chosen first and foremost because of a special ability, a talent for working with entrepreneurs and helping them grow their companies.

Many existing incubators may perceive this vision as a dream. Others will adopt it as their goal and will try to implement the principles and practices laid out in this book. Some will be able to change course more easily than others. New incubators will be able to set their course by using this book to help them determine what is "true north" in their particular situation.

EMERGING TRENDS

While incubators are important, it is actually what happens within incubators, i.e., the business incubation process, that matters. Five trends that will have a major impact on the incubator industry over the next five years are listed below.

Emerging Trends

1. Services to Client Companies Outside the Incubator

2. Incubators Attached to Research/Knowledge Centers

3. Innovation Centers

4. Virtual Incubators

5. Entrepreneurial Support Systems

SERVICES TO CLIENT COMPANIES OUTSIDE THE INCUBATOR

Many incubators already provide support and services to client companies which are not located in the incubators but which want, need and are willing to pay for services the incubator can provide. This trend is increasing. Sometimes the incubator is too small to accommodate all the companies that want to be admitted. Sometimes the companies have developed to the point where they do not need to be in day-to-day contact with the president or other companies. Those who "graduate" from the incubator may still need periodic assistance. Those who were never located in the incubator may want help with strategic issues. Often companies which are "Up-and-Comers" or "rising stars" recognize they need help with issues such as recruiting other members of the management team, filling out their board of directors, developing business strategies and marketing their products to different customers. They seek access to the incubator for its capacities and resources for helping companies grow.

INCUBATORS ATTACHED TO RESEARCH/KNOWLEDGE CENTERS

Federal laboratories are expected to commercialize as much of their technology as possible. One of the challenges they face is finding people who can identify which technology has commercial potential, determining where to market the technology (e.g., industries and companies that might be interested or find the technology useful), deciding what the technology is worth and how to price it, then concluding whether to license the technology or build a company around it.

Universities face the same problem. Only a few have become adept at licensing technology, and even fewer currently have experience with creating companies around a technology. Corporations are also in the process of re-evaluating their shelf technology to determine whether some of these products and processes might have value equal to or greater than the research and development dollars invested in them.

In all three cases, business incubation programs are being created and attached to the research or knowledge center or embedded within companies as a way to facilitate the effective transfer and commercialization of technology—a trend that is expected to continue, even increase.

INNOVATION CENTERS

Incubators provide access to a president who provides assistance and serves as a "switching center" to other resources and expertise and usually a facility within which companies co-locate and share services. Some states and communities are creating next-generation incubators—sometimes termed "innovation centers"—which offer services that extend far beyond what incubators have traditionally been expected to provide. For instance, some innovation centers work closely with university centers of excellence and identify technology that has enough commercial potential to warrant creation of a new company to capitalize on that opportunity. They then license that technology to a company that they create, *de novo*. Other innovation centers assume a portion of the roles and responsibilities of the university's office of technology transfer or technology management. Still other innovation centers not only link companies to possible sources of funds, they actually administer microloan funds, offer seed-capital funds, manage state and SBA loan programs, sponsor investment fairs, and create angel investor networks within their innovation center. This trend is likely to continue, especially in communities that have universities and/or federal labs located nearby.

VIRTUAL INCUBATORS

As federal, state and local governments recognize the important role start-up companies play in achieving a vibrant economy, there is more support for various types of organizations that provide support to small business—in the hopes that many small companies will grow up to become large companies. As a result, there are many more groups providing support to entrepreneurs than ever before, yet entrepreneurs have difficulty finding the person or organization that can advise them about their particular problem. Recently intermediary organizations have been formed to help entrepreneurs sort through the array of support organizations. For example, one organization provides advice, counsel and assistance with business planning to entrepreneurs and then links them to other organizations or people who can help with specific needs. This organization has decided not to offer facilities for the entrepreneurs. In another case, a statewide organization manages offices on three campuses and a statewide database of faculty, organizations and programs that are available to help entrepreneurs grow their companies. Rather than provide services directly, this organization's staff talk with the entrepreneur just enough to assess his/her needs, then accesses the database and sends the entrepreneur to the appropriate resource. In the coming months, the database will be open to anyone with a modem or access to Internet, so entrepreneurs can use the system themselves to ascertain what resources are available to meet their needs.

Although they do not have walls and they do not provide shared business services, these "virtual incubators" play the same role of switching center or linking system that incubators play.

ENTREPRENEURIAL SUPPORT SYSTEMS

There are certainly examples of communities with no incubators and lots of growing companies. Yet more and more communities are recognizing that incubators play a larger role than just housing and facilitating the growth of a few start-up companies. Well-conceived and managed incubators can serve as a focal point for educating students and citizens of all ages about the changing dynamics in our economy; the important role start-up companies play in creating jobs and wealth; and the support structures that small companies need in order to grow large and become successful. Far from creating a haven for companies that cannot exist on their own, incubators provide the special assistance that helps companies grow healthier and faster than they would be able to do on their own. The previous chapter provides insight into the formula for successful business incubation. "Further Readings" provides additional references.

Incubators are catalysts for creating entrepreneurial support systems in communities. The concentration of start-up companies in an incubator makes it easier to recognize the Three Ms that all start-up companies need and help communities develop appropriate resources to meet those needs:

1. Management: people who can start, grow and develop a company. Contrary to what many technologists believe, management is far more important than technology in making or breaking a company. When choosing between first-rate people with second-rate technology and first-rate technology with second-rate people, venture capitalists will

always bet on the former. Alternatively, they may be willing to invest in a company with first-rate technology if they can replace the second-rate people with people more skilled and experienced in growing the company.

2. Marketing: expertise regarding who will buy what products, in what form and for what price

3. Money: sources of capital and knowledge of where to go and how much money to seek for start-up, development, expansion and growth.

But in order to increase the stream of entrepreneurs who can grow and develop companies, programs at the high school, community college and university levels are needed to introduce students to the option of starting their own companies rather than working in a large corporation. Programs involving education and experiential learning, internships and fellowships enable people to work alongside the entrepreneur and learn, firsthand, the agony and ecstasy of growing their own companies. Short-term courses; consultants who serve as master teachers to entrepreneurs on business planning and strategy; and mentorship programs between successful and novice entrepreneurs are all ways entrepreneurs can be helped in the development of their management and marketing skills.

A note of caution is appropriate at this point. Those responsible for achieving the mission of the incubator cannot take responsibility for these activities, nor should these activities distract practicing entrepreneurs from building successful companies. But the incubator can be a catalyst for encouraging other community organizations (schools, universities and colleges, chambers of commerce, business clubs) to develop programs to stimulate the flow of new entrepreneurs into the local economy and to further develop the entrepreneurs already identified.

Entrepreneurs in every community complain about a shortage of capital—debt or equity—which they need in order to grow their companies. Incubator boards and presidents can use their client companies as case examples in their effort to educate the community about the need for a full array of financing programs to support start-up and growing companies— from seed and early stage through expansion capital, from micro-loans to equity. Banks are often reluctant to loan money to start-up companies whose only asset is their intellectual property—which a banker cannot see, touch or smell. Admission to and location in an incubator makes the company more credible and makes a loan more plausible. Over time the bankers, accountants, lawyers and others gain experience and increased comfort with start-up companies in general, because of their successful experiences with companies located in or affiliated with the incubator.

Granted, it takes a talented and persistent incubator president to educate, coach and cajole entrepreneurs to make the right moves and decisions necessary to grow their companies. It also requires an unusual board and supportive stakeholders to launch and develop a successful incubator.

Stakeholders, board members and presidents who choose to develop a best practices incubator should be able to see a much stronger entrepreneurial support system throughout the community within five to eight years.

This book was written to provide a new direction to the incubator industry. Rather than describe common practices, the cases illustrate what happens when best practices are followed: a healthy, prosperous incubator and successful companies. For those involved in the incubator industry, this book provides guideposts and a road map.

The incubator's mission is the development of companies; everything else is secondary to that primary mission. A best practices incubator is managed like a business. It focuses as many resources as possible on the development of the client companies and minimizes the resources spent on general and administrative functions. Differentiated programs and services are delivered to companies according to their individualized needs and stages of development.

Implementing the principles and practices of successful business incubation will lead to more successful entrepreneurs growing more successful new ventures creating more new jobs—and that will result in more self-sufficient people and healthy communities.

Profiles of Successful Incubator Presidents & Directors

LAURA J. KILCREASE
Austin Technology Incubator

Ms. Kilcrease has more than 16 years in many aspects of high-technology business, including hardware, software and technology services. She was educated in the United Kingdom as a Chartered Management Accountant and earned her MBA at The University of Texas at Austin.

Her career includes tenure as a key member of Control Data Corporation's financial team. Her extensive international experience encompasses activities in Europe, the Pacific Rim and the United States. She has used her organizational and management skills in handling the acquisition, merger, and sale of major business units within large Fortune 100 companies and has also applied her talents to small start-up technology companies.

Ms. Kilcrease was recruited to help launch and then direct the Austin Technology Incubator by executives of the RGK Foundation, one of whom was impressed by her performance at a videotaped community networking meeting.

She currently serves as the Director of Commercialization and Enterprise activities for the IC^2 Institute at The University of Texas at Austin. These activities include the Austin Software Council, the UT Austin Entrepreneurs' Council, the Texas Capital Network, the Austin Technology Incubator (ATI) and two NASA technology commercialization centers, one at the Ames Research Center in California and the other at the Johnson Space Center in Houston, Texas.

She has provided the leadership for ATI, an innovative technology commercialization incubator, since its inception in 1989. ATI has nurtured more than 38 fledging companies, created more than 550 jobs and brought in excess of $60 million to the Austin community during its first four years of operation.

According to Ms. Kilcrease: "An incubator president needs three key talents: (1) the capacity to communicate with all different kinds of people in all different kinds of circumstances; (2) the ability to multiplex, i.e., to successfully juggle many balls simultaneously; and (3) a personality that thrives on crisis management, since one-third of all small businesses are in crisis mode at all times."

SUSAN MATLOCK
Birmingham Business Assistance Network

Susan Matlock has public and private sector experience. During six years as Assistant to the Mayor of Birmingham and as Director of Community Development for the Metropolitan Development Board, Ms. Matlock gained extensive experience in recruiting businesses to Birmingham and accommodating businesses that were growing. In addition, she learned to access funding sources to support business development. She had private sector work experience as well, including three years as a bank lending officer.

In the mid 1980s, the City of Birmingham and the business leadership in the community were working together to determine the feasibility of establishing a service and light-manufacturing business incubation program. Recognizing Ms. Matlock's track record and expertise, two of the community leaders who would become founding members of the Board of Directors of the new organization contacted Ms. Matlock about setting up the program. Her public and private background seemed particularly appropriate, as did her lending experience. Her experience in the Mayor's Office in capital budgeting and economic development was viewed as an asset with respect to fundraising for both the incubator and its companies. Her public and private experience would also provide a strong foundation for building an effective community network. Initially under a six-month contract as Birmingham Project Manager for Control Data Corporation, Ms. Matlock established a management assistance program for entrepreneurs, an organization of volunteer professional advisers and a not-for-profit seed equity and loan fund.

In 1986, Ms. Matlock was selected to head the Birmingham Business Assistance Network, a 501(c)(3) economic development agency that includes the management of the business incubation center. Her success has been recognized through her award in 1989 as SBA Financial Services Advocate of the Year for Alabama.

Ms. Matlock comments: "In my view, it is critical that those responsible for developing a business incubation program realize that they are themselves acting as entrepreneurs. They are developing a new business that must meet all the market and financial tests that any emerging business must meet. A business incubation program should not be launched without fully developing a business plan that includes not only an annual operating budget complete with sources and uses of funds but also the same month-by-month cash flow projections for the first two years that would be expected of any other new business. It is extremely unwise to receive initial funding commitments and start spending money to develop a business incubation program without a long-term view of the program's financial viability. As with a business, underplanning can lead to the failure of the business incubation program."

ROBERT MEEDER
SPEDD

Bob Meeder came to the incubator business with experience in administration and teaching in a community college and as a hospital research director. He also worked as a fund-raising and grant-writing consultant to public agencies regarding small business development. Both consulting and fundraising would prove to be very helpful skills as an incubator developer and manager. While serving as Executive Dean and Interim President of a community college, Bob pursued a Ph.D. degree at the University of Pittsburgh, completing his dissertation: *Business Incubation as a Community Service Function of University Programming*. That research effort catalyzed Dr. Meeder's departure from academia and launched his career in business incubation.

Dr. Meeder is currently President of SPEDD, Inc., which operates the nation's largest network of business incubators in Pennsylvania and Ohio. SPEDD currently has affiliate centers in Slovenia and Hungary and is in the process of establishing additional affiliates in California, Michigan, Ohio and Connecticut. Over the course of his past dozen years in this field, SPEDD has developed the most extensive business management assistance program in the country, with over forty office-practice, technical and management services. Dr. Meeder is also a partner in the Brackenridge Corporation, which provides comprehensive economic development and business development services to municipalities, universities and private companies throughout the United States, Canada and Europe.

According to Dr. Meeder: "Entrepreneurs tend to seek management assistance when they are in major or minor crisis mode. The incubator president, on the other hand, must take a proactive approach and must continually offer services before an entrepreneur is even aware that he/she needs them. This is the only way to counteract the entrepreneur's crisis, knee-jerk request for too much help in too little time—conditions that minimize the probability of the president being effective."

JULIUS MORGAN
Milwaukee Enterprise Center (MEC)

Julius Morgan has experience in both the public and private sectors in (1) computer systems, (2) development of financial, project-management and inventory systems, and (3) management of teams. In his positions in the public sector and a utility, he had the opportunity to interact extensively with small business. In addition to his business experience, Mr. Morgan has had a long and positive experience as a community activist. His track record in community affairs and his capacity to catalyze and sustain communication among disparate groups was as important as his business experience in making him the top choice of incubator sponsors for the position. His knowledge of the business start-up process and his access to the community network have been valuable resources for the MEC client companies. Finally, his former employers were also major sponsors of the incubator project, which reassured all the sponsors that the MEC would have competent management and a powerful advocate.

Reflecting on his success in the early days of establishing the MEC, Mr. Morgan stated: "With the help of the MEC sponsors, I was able to secure significant financial investments for launching our incubator. When a number of community service groups lined up to lay claim to their piece of the pie, I was successful in standing up to them and saying, 'No, these funds will be used to support the development of new businesses, which in turn will be the source of new jobs. That is the best service we can provide for our community.' Although there was initial resistance to my position, eventually the community service organizations pulled together to become a significant part of the stakeholder support network for the MEC."

ROBERT J. SHERWOOD
Center for Business Innovation

As president of the Center for Business Innovation (CBI) in Kansas City, Bob Sherwood leads an organization dedicated to starting and accelerating the growth of emerging businesses. The Center for Business Innovation currently has ownership interests in 37 companies engaged in the fields of computer hardware, software, manufacturing, medicine and telecommunications. The National Business Incubation Association selected CBI as the 1993 Incubator of the Year.

Mr. Sherwood has personal experience with starting and growing companies. He was a founding officer of RasterOps Corporation, a firm which manufactures and markets products for high-resolution color and computer imaging applications. In five years, the company achieved sales of $100 million, grew to 400 employees, and became publicly traded. He was an executive with Envirotech Corporation, which grew from $2 million to over $500 million in six years, and was also a founder and President of EDC, a $10 million environmental-equipment manufacturing company. *Fortune* magazine named EDC one of the ten most innovative small companies in California. After his considerable success as an entrepreneur in Silicon Valley, Mr. Sherwood returned home to Kansas City to be near family. Soon after, he was recruited by key sponsors of the CBI to assume the leadership role as president.

Mr. Sherwood offers insights for both incubator presidents and incubator entrepreneurs:

"For most companies that fail, the entrepreneur quits too soon. Persistence and commitment overcome many barriers. By associating with an incubator, the company increases its valuation, decreases its start-up costs, and increases its probability of success. It's important to understand that the incubator building is a very minor part of the incubator's array of services—a necessary evil for being able to provide assistance with the 'Three Ms'—marketing, management and money—to client entrepreneurs. For most of the people I talk with, this is truly a paradigm shift in thinking. They think the building is the incubator, but nothing could be farther from the truth. If we can make the jump into hyperspace, then whole new vistas of entrepreneurial assistance take shape."

Further Readings

ENTREPRENEURS AND ENTREPRENEURSHIP

Hisrich, Robert D. and Peters, Michael P. *Entrepreneurship.* Chicago, Illinois: Irwin, 1995. Englewood Cliffs, New Jersey: Prentice Hall, 1990.

Kuratko, Donald F. and Hodgetts, Richard M. *Entrepreneurship: A Contemporary Approach.* Second Edition. Fort Worth, Texas: The Dryden Press, 1992.

Roberts, Edward B. *Entrepreneurs in High Technology: Lessons from MIT and Beyond.* New York, NY: Oxford University Press, 1991.

Sahlman, William A. and Stevenson, Howard H. *The Entrepreneurial Venture.* Boston, Massachusetts: Harvard Business School Publications, 1992.

Sexton, Donald L. and Kasarda, John D. *The State of the Art of Entrepreneurship.* Boston, Massachusetts: PWS-KENT Publishing Company, 1992

Sexton, Donald L. and Upton, Nancy. *Entrepreneurship: Creativity & Growth.* New York, NY: MacMillan, 1991.

Stevenson, Howard H.; Roberts, Michael J.; and Grousbeck, H. Irving. *New Business Ventures and the Entrepreneur.* 4th Edition. Homewood, Illinois: Irwin, 1994.

Timmons, Jeffry A. *New Venture Creation.* 4th Edition. Burr Ridge, Illinois: Irwin, 1994.

Vesper, Karl H. *New Venture Experience.* Seattle, Washington: Vector Books, 1994.

VENTURE FINANCING

Bygrave, William D. and Timmons, Jeffry A. *Venture Capital at the Crossroads.* Boston, Massachusetts: Harvard Business School Press, 1992.

Rich, Stanley R. and Gumpert, David E. *Business Plans that Win $$.* New York, NY: Harper & Row, 1985.

CORPORATE ENTREPRENEURSHIP

Block, Zenus and MacMillan, Ian C. *Corporate Venturing*. Boston, Massachusetts: Harvard Business School Press, 1993.

Botkin, James W. and Matthews, Jana B. *Winning Combinations—The Coming Wave of Entrepreneurial Partnerships Between Large & Small Companies*. New York, NY: John Wiley & Sons, Inc., 1992.

Drucker, Peter F. *Innovation and Entrepreneurship*. New York, NY: Harper & Row, 1993.

Kanter, Rosabeth. *When Giants Learn to Dance*. New York, NY: Simon and Schuster, 1989.

Morone, Joseph G. *Winning in High Tech Markets*. Boston, Massachusetts: Harvard Business School Press, 1993.

INCUBATOR OPERATIONS

Bearse, Peter. *The Evaluation of Business Incubation Projects: A Comprehensive Manual*. Athens, Ohio: National Business Incubation Association, 1994.

Campbell, Candace. *Change Agents in the New Economy: Business Incubators and Economic Development*. Athens, Ohio: National Business Incubation Association, 1992.

Meeder, Robert A. *Forging the Incubator: How to Design and Implement a Feasibility Study for a Business Incubation Program*. Athens, Ohio: National Business Incubation Association, 1993.

NBIA. *The State of the Business Incubation Industry, 1991*. Athens, Ohio: National Business Incubation Association, 1992.

NBIA. *Applying for Internal Revenue Code Section 501(c)3 or Similar Tax Exempt Status*. Athens, Ohio: National Business Incubation Association, 1990.

NBIA. *Bricks and Mortar: How to Find and Design the Best Business Incubation Facilities*. Athens, Ohio: National Business Incubation Association, 1992.

NBIA. *Business Incubator Marketing Strategies*. Athens, Ohio: National Business Incubation Association, 1990.

NBIA. *Human Resources: In Search of Incubator Management*. Athens, Ohio: National Business Incubation Association, 1994.

NBIA. *Leases, Policies and Applications for Not-for-Profit Incubators*. Athens, Ohio: National Business Incubation Association, 1990.

NBIA. *The State of the Business Incubation Industry, 1991*. Athens, Ohio: National Business Incubation Association, 1992.

Smilor, Raymond W. and Gill, Michael D. Jr. *The New Business Incubator: Linking Talent, Technology, Capital and Know-How*. New York, NY: Free Press, 1986.

Index

About the Authors

Dr. Jana B. Matthews is Senior Research and Teaching Fellow and Director of Entrepreneur Support Systems Programs at the Center for Entrepreneurial Leadership Inc. at the Ewing Marion Kauffman Foundation in Kansas City. She is responsible for programs, projects and grants to achieve best practices in incubators and innovation centers; more effective transfer and commercialization of technology; development of more seed and early stage capital programs; and the creation of entrepreneurial infrastructures in communities.

She was the founding president of two start-up companies: NCHEMS Management Services, Inc., and M&H Group, Inc., a consulting firm specializing in technology-based economic development with an international clientele. She was also a member of the senior staff of Arthur D. Little in Cambridge, Massachusetts.

Dr. Matthews has an undergraduate degree from Earlham College, studied at the University of London, Yale University, the Harvard Business School, the Sloan School of Management, and has a doctorate from Harvard University.

She was a gubernatorial appointee to the Colorado Advanced Technology Institute and served on the Board of Directors of the Association of University-Related Research Parks and the Boulder Technology Incubator. She has co-authored several books, including *Effective Use of Management Consultants in Higher Education, Managing the Partnership Between Higher Education and Industry* and *Winning Combinations: The Coming Wave of Entrepreneurial Partnerships Between Large and Small Companies.*

Dr. Mark P. Rice is a veteran of the business incubation industry. In 1979, he co-founded Power Kinetics, an outgrowth of a solar energy research project at Rensselaer Polytechnic Institute (RPI). Power Kinetics was one of the first companies to join the Rensselaer Incubator Program after its founding in late 1980. In 1988, after four years in the field of business and investment brokerage, Dr. Rice returned to Rensselaer to become the Director of the Incubator Program. Within a year he doubled the number of participating companies, co-founded the Center for Entrepreneurship of New Technological Ventures within the School of Management, and launched the Venture Affiliates of RPI, a network of sixty regional entrepreneurial ventures.

In 1989, Rice was elected to the first of two terms on the board of directors of the National Business Incubation Association, for which he served as Chairman from 1990 to 1992. He has consulted with incubator developers throughout the United States and Mexico, Columbia, Chile, Poland, Ukraine, Indonesia, Malaysia and Singapore. Dr. Rice also founded the annual Rensselaer Alumni Entrepreneur of the Year Celebration in 1990, which has become the focal point for an extensive network of highly successful entrepreneurial alumni who support Rensselaer's entrepreneurship initiatives. In 1992 he was selected to be one of twelve Executive Advisers for the newly formed Center for Entrepreneurial Leadership Inc. at the Ewing Marion Kauffman Foundation.

Currently, Dr. Rice is the Director of the Center for Entrepreneurship of New Technological Ventures (CENTV) at Rensselaer, recognized by *Business Week* and *Success* magazines as one of the top entrepreneurship programs in the country. CENTV is one of nine member institutions of the National Consortium of Centers of Entrepreneurship, founded in 1995 under the sponsorship of the Center for Entrepreneurial Leadership Inc. Rice continues to serve as Executive Director of the Incubator and Assistant Dean in the School of Management. He has B.S. and M.S. degrees in Mechanical Engineering and a Ph.D. in Management, all from Rensselaer Polytechnic Institute. His Ph.D. dissertation research focused on in-depth field studies of ten incubators and was titled: *Intervention Mechanisms Used to Influence the Critical Success Factors of New Ventures: An Exploratory Study.*

DATE DUE			
OCT 2 0 1997			